D1411992

EGYPT

TITLES IN THE MODERN NATIONS OF THE WORLD SERIES INCLUDE:

Canada
China
Cuba
Egypt
England
Germany
Ireland
Italy
Mexico
Russia
Somalia
South Korea

EGYPT

BY STUART A. KALLEN

LUCENT BOOKS
P.O. BOX 289011
SAN DIEGO, CA 92198-9011

T 32371   Egypt

Library of Congress Cataloging-in-Publication Data

Kallen, Stuart A.
    Egypt / by Stuart A. Kallen.
       p.   cm. — (Modern nations of the world)
    Includes bibliographical references (p.   ) and index.
    Summary: Discusses the history, geography, people, and culture of
Egypt and its significance in the world today.
    ISBN 1-56006-535-4 (lib. : alk. paper)
    1. Egypt—Juvenile literature. [1. Egypt.] I. Title. II. Series.
DT49.F67   1999
962—dc21   98-43851
                                                     CIP
                                                      AC

No part of this book may be reproduced or used in any form or by any means, electrical, mechanical, or otherwise, including, but not limited to, photocopy, recording, or any information storage and retrieval system, without prior written permission from the publisher.

Copyright © 1999 by Lucent Books, Inc.
P.O. Box 289011, San Diego, CA 92198-9011
Printed in the U.S.A.

CONTENTS

INTRODUCTION   6
Egypt: Crossroads of the World

CHAPTER ONE   8
Geography and Population

CHAPTER TWO   20
Ancient History

CHAPTER THREE   36
Egypt Under Foreign Rule

CHAPTER FOUR   49
Creating an Identity

CHAPTER FIVE   65
Daily Life and Culture

CHAPTER SIX   79
Challenges Today and Tomorrow

Facts About Egypt   91
Notes   95
Chronology   97
Suggestions for Further Reading   101
Works Consulted   103
Index   105
Picture Credits   111
About the Author   111

INTRODUCTION

EGYPT: CROSSROADS OF THE WORLD

Egypt is located on a geographical bridge that links Africa and Asia. It is also an heir to a civilization that dates back more than six thousand years. By 3000 B.C. Egypt was one of the most powerful countries in the world, possessing highly developed government and religious institutions.

The pyramids and other monuments from that era still survive today. These tombs and temples were originally built by Egyptian kings, called pharaohs, to aid their journey into the afterlife when they died. The pyramids provide living proof in the modern world of the advanced mathematical, astronomical, and architectural skills practiced by ancient Egypt's scholars.

Almost twenty-five hundred years ago the Greek historian Herodotus wrote about Egypt: "Nowhere are there so many marvelous things, nor in the whole world are there to be seen so many things of unspeakable greatness."[1]

Egypt's strategic location between the African, European, and Asian continents has caused the country to be the subject of numerous conquests. Over the centuries, Egypt has been occupied by Greek, Roman, Arabian, Turkish, French, British, and other peoples. Egypt has also been a place of religious conflict, with Christians, Jews, and Islamic sects clashing throughout the ages.

Egypt's Suez Canal, which opened in 1869, links Africa to Asia and permits oceangoing vessels to travel between the eastern end of the Mediterranean Sea and the Indian Ocean via the Gulf of Suez and the Red Sea. This strategic canal has also proved to be a point of contention throughout the years.

A CULTURAL CROSSROADS

In spite of the struggles, Egypt has the longest cultural history of any country in the world. People have lived along the Nile River since about 5200 B.C. Ancient Egyptian culture influenced the Hebrew and Greek civilizations as well as the Christians and Muslims.

Modern Egypt is a place of contrasts and a cultural crossroads between East and West, ancient and modern. Mud-and-brick villages stand beside four-thousand-year-old pyramids, which are located a few miles from glass-and-steel office and apartment buildings. Television antennae sprout from rooftops in Cairo while farmers throughout the Nile's fertile valley tend their fields with the ancient tools of their ancestors. Camera-toting tourists from all over the world flock to the pyramids in their athletic shoes while religious worshipers follow the ancient call to prayer in long flowing robes.

Through everything, the Nile River flows silently. The river has been Egypt's lifeblood since the beginning of history, and it is the waterway that provides the country with its important link to the twenty-first century.

The great pyramids are living proof of the advanced mathematical, astronomical, and architectural skills of ancient Egyptian scholars.

1

GEOGRAPHY AND POPULATION

Egypt's formal name is the Arab Republic of Egypt, and its capital city is Cairo. The country is 386,661 square miles in area, approximately the size of Colorado, Utah, Arizona, and New Mexico combined. Nearly all of Egypt is on the continent of Africa. The Sinai Peninsula in Egypt's northeast corner is the only part of the country that lies in Asia. The Suez Canal marks the dividing line between the two continents. Egypt is bordered on the west by Libya, on the south by Sudan, on the north by the Mediterranean Sea, and on the east by Israel and the Red Sea. Across the Red Sea lies the oil-rich country of Saudi Arabia.

Egypt lies on the eastern edge of the vast, empty, and arid region called the Sahara, whose very name in Arabic means "desert." Egypt is composed of four major regions: the Nile Valley and Delta, the Western Desert, the Eastern Desert, and the Sinai Peninsula. The area of higher elevation in the south of the country is called Upper Egypt and the Upper Nile; the lower area in the north is called Lower Egypt and the Lower Nile. Less than 24,800 square miles of Egypt's 386,661 square miles will support human life and agriculture.

Ninety-six percent of Egypt is desert. The Western Desert, which makes up two-thirds of the country, is a vast area of sands rippled by shifting winds. In some areas the sand piles up into huge dunes. The Qattara Depression in northwestern Egypt is a sunken area that lies 436 feet below sea level.

The Eastern Desert is also called the Arabian Desert. Long ago, before the Red Sea existed, this desert was connected to the Arabian Peninsula. The Eastern Desert slopes up gently into rocky hills east of the Nile. Deep ravines that cut into this area are called *wadis*.

Although the Sahara has long been an inhospitable desert, modern satellite pictures have shown that a vast network of old river beds exist below its surface. Cave paintings in the area have also proven that as recently as four thousand years ago the Sahara was a fertile area teeming with a rich variety of fish and animal life in its rivers and green valleys.

THE NILE RIVER

Although most of Egypt is a desert, the life-giving Nile River has provided Egypt's people with a source of survival for thousands of years. The Nile—the world's longest river—has played a major role in the creation of Egypt's geography in a process that started 5 million years ago, when the river began to flow northward from two sources in Ethiopia (the Blue Nile) and Uganda (the White Nile). The rivers met in modern-day Khartoum, Sudan.

The White Nile is the longest branch of the river. From the source of the White Nile to the Mediterranean Sea, the Nile River is 4,145 miles long. Near Cairo the Nile fans out into scores of streams that empty into the Mediterranean. This area is called the Nile Delta, after the Greek letter that looks like a triangle. The Nile Delta is about 100 miles long from north to south and about 160 miles wide along the coast.

The Nile flows through Egypt for about 950 miles. In centuries past the river was much wider and was bordered by marshland and swamps. Gradually the river deepened and narrowed, carrying vast quantities of gravel, sand, and silt, called alluvium, to the mouth of the river. This formed the huge delta and created what was to become the most fertile area of Egypt. Because of the rich soil, the ancient Egyptians called this land Kemet, meaning "Black Land." They called the surrounding desert Deshret, or "Red Land."

Almost every July torrential summer rains in Ethiopia's highlands poured into the Blue Nile, causing the river's waters to rise in Egypt. By August the Nile was in full flood. This was called "the Inundation" by the ancient Egyptians. When the floodwaters receded at the end of October, they left behind silt and mud, which spread out from the riverbanks in amounts that equaled about four inches per century. The receding waters also left behind lagoons and

THE SUEZ CANAL

The Suez Canal is located at the crossroads of Asia, Europe, and Africa. Owned and operated by Egypt, the canal is one of the most important waterways in the world. The Suez Canal crosses the narrow Isthmus of Suez, joining Africa and Asia. It permits ocean vessels to travel between the eastern end of the Mediterranean Sea and the Indian Ocean via the Red Sea. The canal has a length of 105 miles and handles about sixty vessels each day. The total transit time averages about fifteen hours.

The canal's strategic importance may be understood when looking at the distances European ships must travel to reach the Far East. For example, were it not for the Suez Canal, a ship sailing from London to Bombay, India, would have to travel 12,400 miles around the continent of Africa. The distance via the canal is 42 percent shorter, averaging 7,270 miles.

In the early 1960s, 15 percent of all world trade moved through the canal; petroleum from the Persian Gulf accounted for 75 percent of the canal's business. By the 1980s giant supertankers and long-distance oil pipelines drastically reduced the percentage of oil going through the Suez Canal.

The present water route between the two oceans was preceded as early as four thousand years ago by a canal from the Nile to the Red Sea. This was filled in for military purposes in A.D. 775. In 1854 Ferdinand-Marie de Lesseps obtained rights to establish a company to build and operate the canal for ninety-nine years. Construction was completed in 1869 at a cost of $41.9 million. The United Kingdom acquired a controlling interest in the canal in 1875. Egyptian president Gamal Abdel Nasser reclaimed the canal for Egypt in 1956.

streams, which became natural reservoirs for fish, birds, and other wildlife. By April the Nile was at its lowest level. Vegetation began to die, the seasonal pools dried up, and game began to move south. When the rains came in July, the process would begin again.

By the twentieth century the fertile soil along the Nile had reached an average depth of about thirty feet. This fertile floodplain was filled in with thickets of trees such as tamarisk, sycamore, and acacia. The soil also supported grasses and other vegetation.

The deposit of alluvium is believed to have started in about 8000 B.C. and continued for about ten thousand years, until 1960. At that time the government of Egypt built the hydroelectric Aswan High Dam, which disrupted the natural flow of the Nile.

Egypt receives little annual rainfall, except in the north on the Mediterranean coast, and the Nile provides vital drinking and irrigation water to the Egyptians. In drought years when the Nile failed to flood, the people of Egypt were stricken with hardship and starvation.

THE ASWAN DAM

The idea of damming the Nile was first proposed in the late 1800s. At that time engineers discovered that during Inundation, between July and October, over 40 percent of the river's water flowed into the Mediterranean before it could be used by the Egyptians. If some method of retaining this water could be devised, the water could be stored until spring and used to irrigate crops when the Nile was at its lowest level.

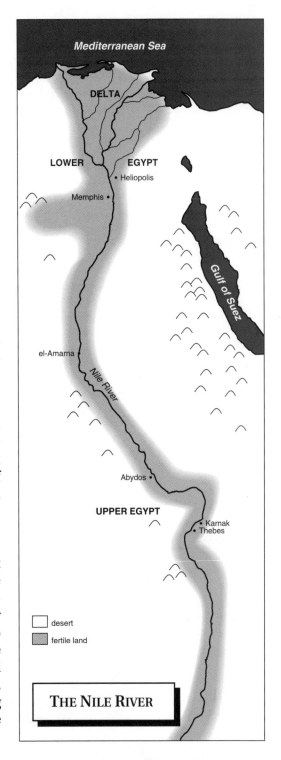

Mediterranean Sea

DELTA

LOWER EGYPT
• Heliopolis

Memphis •

el-Amarna

Nile River

Gulf of Suez

Abydos •

UPPER EGYPT

• Karnak
• Thebes

☐ desert
▨ fertile land

THE NILE RIVER

In the 1890s a British engineer designed a dam across the Nile at Aswan, 620 miles south of Cairo. The dam was more than 1 mile long, 90 feet high, and 90 feet thick. It was designed with 180 sluice gates at its base, which would allow the alluvium to flow down the Nile as it had for millennia. Work began on the Aswan Dam in 1898, and the project was completed four years later on December 10, 1902.

By the 1960s Egypt's government wanted to utilize even more of the Nile's waters and also use the river to generate

OASES

An area of the desert where water flows underground is called an oasis. In the Western Desert oases are marked by water gushing up into pools and ponds surrounded by date palm trees and lush gardens. Some oases are used to irrigate rich green valleys. Oases that flow near the Nile are known as New Valley oases. In ages past these areas were fed by branches of the Nile.

Oasis water is rich in sulfur and other minerals and is valued for its health benefits. People come from all over the world to bathe in oasis water. Likewise, the silt that sinks to the bottom is used to treat stomach, skin, bone, muscle, and other health problems.

Tribes of Bedouins who still wander the desert depend on oases for survival for themselves and their goats, sheep, and camels.

An oasis means survival for tribes that herd their goats, sheep, and camels in the desert.

The Aswan High Dam has allowed 900,000 acres of desert to become irrigated farmland.

power. On January 9, 1960, construction began on the Aswan High Dam, four miles upstream from the old Aswan Dam. The Aswan High Dam was designed by engineers in the Soviet Union and was dedicated on January 15, 1971. The dam cost over $1 billion to build.

The Aswan High Dam is one of the world's largest structures, stretching 2.3 miles in length and rising 364 feet above the riverbed. The dam has a hydroelectric capacity that provides Egypt with 25 percent of its electrical power. The water stored by the dam allowed 900,000 acres of former desert to become irrigated for farmland. It also provided irrigation that allowed crops to be grown year round.

The Aswan High Dam created Lake Nasser, which is about 312 miles long and extends across Egypt's border into Sudan. When engineers realized that the creation of Lake Nasser would flood ancient monuments such as the temple Abu Simbel and the temple of Philae, thousands of engineers and laborers from all over the world formed a rescue team to save the monuments. They were taken apart stone by stone and moved to higher ground, where they were reassembled. This massive task took ten years.

For all its benefits, the Aswan High Dam has its drawbacks. It traps the silt from the river in Lake Nasser, so the Nile Valley no longer gets natural fertilizer. And without the Nile's gushing force, saltwater from the Mediterranean flows into the Nile Delta, poisoning the water for wildlife.

CITIES AND TOWNS

About 99 percent of Egypt's population lives along the Nile or beside the Suez Canal, making these areas among the most densely populated living spaces in the world. In the mid-1990s

EGYPTIAN ANIMALS

The waters of Egypt are home to a wide variety of animals. Long-legged herons and other birds feed on fish along the banks of the Nile. Gulls, ospreys, and spoonbills nest along the Red Sea. Lake Nasser is a haven for migrating birds, including pelicans, geese, terns, plovers, and warblers, and crocodiles swim along the lake's banks. On the Sinai Peninsula a species of wild mountain goat called the ibex runs across the steep, rocky slopes of the desert.

The most famous animal in Egypt is probably the camel. Camels are seen on city streets and in desert wastelands, and they are called "ships of the desert" because they can travel several weeks through oceans of sand without needing water. Egypt's camels are dromedaries, or one-humped camels. They store fat, not water, in their hump. After a long period without water, a camel can drink twenty-five gallons without stopping.

Another famous creature in Egypt is the scarab, or dung beetle. Scarabs crawl along pushing a huge ball of dung, or animal manure. To ancient Egyptians, the scarab represented Khepri, the god of the dawning sun. Khepri was believed to push the sun across the darkness so that it could rise the next day. Images of scarabs are used in Egypt as good luck charms and jewelry.

Cats were first domesticated and used for pets in Egypt. They were sacred animals to the ancient Egyptians, who believed they represented the goddess Bast, daughter of the sun god Re. Because of their status, cats were mummified and buried in special cat cemeteries. Today thousands of wild cats live in the Nile Delta.

The scarab beetle, also known as the dung beetle, represents Khepri, the god of the dawning sun.

Egypt had a population of more than 61 million, making it the second most populated country in Africa after Nigeria.

There is a saying in Egypt: "Every minute in Cairo, one person is born and two more arrive by train."[2] That expression is derived from the fact that Cairo, founded in the tenth century, is Egypt's largest city with more than 15 million people living in and around the Greater Cairo area. Alexandria, Egypt's second largest city with a population of 3.3 million, was founded in 332 B.C. by the conqueror Alexander the Great. Today it is a busy port on the Mediterranean. Giza, a suburb of Cairo, is the site of three pyramids and the Great Sphinx. Port Said, Egypt's fourth largest city with a population of 400,000, was founded in 1860 on the site where engineers began building the Suez Canal. Today it is a major port.

With more than 15 million people, Cairo reigns as Egypt's largest city.

One of Egypt's oldest cities is Luxor, which was originally the ancient city of Thebes. Luxor is famous for its many temples and tombs, including the Luxor Temple, the temple of Karnak, and the pyramid-filled Valley of the Kings.

The desolate areas of the Western and Eastern Deserts are marked by oases, isolated green areas with underground wells. Smaller communities cluster around each desert oasis. The Egyptian government has tried to attract more settlers to these rural areas, but the allure of jobs and money continues to draw people to large cities.

THE PEOPLE OF EGYPT

Anthropologists divide the Egyptian people into three racial groups. The largest group is the Hamito-Semitic race that has lived along the Nile for millennia. This group includes the Berbers, who settled in the western part of the country around Siwa. The second group of Egyptians is descended from Arabs, particularly the Bedouin Arab nomads who migrated to the country from Arabia. The third group are the Nubians, who originally lived in the Aswan area.

Over the years native Egyptians have mixed with a wide variety of people who have traded in or conquered their country. These include Ethiopians, Persians, Turks, Central Asians, Greeks, Romans, French, and British.

Members of Egypt's largest minority group are called Coptic Christians, or Copts, and they are a religious rather than ethnic minority. Copts are direct descendants of Egyptians who lived during the time of the pharaohs.

The Bedouins are some of the world's most isolated people, living around wells or oases, traveling on camels, and living in goatskin tents.

In the seventh century Arabs invaded Egypt, which was then a Christian country. After the Arab conquest the Copts formed a Christian majority. Over time, however, many Copts converted to Islam. Today the Egyptian government estimates that about 2 million Copts live in Egypt. The Copts say their numbers are higher: between 6 and 7 million.

An estimated 350,000 Greeks constitute Egypt's largest non-Arab minority. Greeks have lived in Egypt for centuries.

BEDOUINS, BERBERS, AND NUBIANS

Egypt is home to nearly five hundred thousand Bedouins who belong to fourteen different tribes. For centuries the Bedouins have lived in the harshest, most isolated parts of the Eastern and Western Deserts and the Sinai Peninsula. Bedouins continue to live in the traditional manner of their ancestors, traveling on camels and living in goatskin tents. To protect themselves from the searing heat, Bedouins wear loose-fitting, layered robes and cloth headdresses. Their livelihood depends on sheep, goats, and camels. Bedouins camp around wells or oases and move on whenever the water supply dries up.

Bedouins have long been known for their warm treatment of guests. An example of this hospitality was published in the 1836 book by Edward William Lane, *An Account of the Manners and Customs of the Modern Egyptians:*

> [Here is] a perfect picture of the manner in which a modern Bedawee (Bedouin) sheykh received travellers arriving at his encampment. He immediately [asks] his wife or women to make bread; slaughters a sheep or some other animal, and dresses it in haste; and bringing milk and any other provisions that he may have ready at hand, with the bread, and the meat which he has dressed, sets them before his guest. If these be persons of high rank, he stands by them while they eat. . . . Most Bedawees will suffer almost any injury to themselves or their families rather than allow their guests to be ill-treated while under their protection.[3]

When this passage was written, the Bedouins were some of the world's most isolated people. In modern times, however, encroaching civilization has begun to affect the traditional lifestyles of the Bedouins. The oases in the Western Desert have been slated for massive agricultural development and resettlement to ease overcrowding in urban areas. Sinai has also been marked for tourist and agricultural development.

The influx of outsiders has forced many Bedouins to completely abandon their traditional lifestyles. Some drive taxis or lead tourists on camel treks through the desert. Today Bedouins may be found living in settlements of crude cement huts or palm-frond shacks with corrugated roofs and TV antennae on top.

About 160,000 Nubians, who are practicing Muslims, live in Egypt. Most Nubians live in cities and urban areas. In the past Nubians lived in villages along the Nile from Aswan south to Sudan. Their traditional lifestyle depended on farming, fishing, and transporting goods up and down the Nile. The lives of the Nubians remained unchanged for centuries until the Aswan High Dam was built. As the water rose behind the dam, it flooded the traditional homeland of the Nubians. As many as 60,000 Nubians were displaced and forced to move to Cairo, Alexandria, and elsewhere.

The Berbers are another minority who have lived the same way for centuries. About six thousand Berbers live in the Western Desert near the border with Libya. The largest Berber community lives in Siwa Oasis. Berbers are Muslims, but they have their own language, which is not related to Arabic. They also have their own unique cultural practices. Berber women usually wear head-to-toe garments, called *melayas*, that have slits for their eyes.

A Berber woman peers through a slit in her melaya, *a traditional head-to-toe garment.*

A GROWING COUNTRY

Egypt's population continues to grow by about 1 million people per year, with city residents greatly outnumbering desert dwellers. The exploding population has created problems of poverty, unemployment, housing shortages, and poor nutrition. The government has slowed growth slightly by providing programs for family planning and birth control. These efforts, however, are opposed by conservative religious factions.

The government has also built housing complexes on the outskirts of Cairo to attract people to less populated areas. But it is difficult to draw people away from the opportunities and entertainment offered by the city. In one unique program to ease overcrowding, women are given five acres of desert land, along with a house and an income, in hopes that men will follow them out to the countryside.

Government officials continue with plans to slow Egypt's growth. In 1994 the United Nations held its International Conference on Population and Development in Cairo. Those attending the conference agreed that the key to population control was educating women and improving their status. In 1997 Egypt held another international population conference to discuss how to balance population growth with natural resources.

With modern problems never envisioned by the pharaohs, Egypt continues to thrive and change, with one eye cast on the ancient pyramids and another looking toward the next century.

2

ANCIENT HISTORY

The roots of civilization in Egypt date back more than nine thousand years. Egyptians have a unique cultural unity and a strong sense of pride in their heritage as one of humankind's earliest civilizations.

People were farming along the banks of the Nile as early as 7000 B.C. The bond between the Nile and the Egyptian people was very strong. Because of the river's rise and fall and subsequent cycle of birth and death, it is easy to understand why the Egyptians were some of the first people to believe in life after death. The fall of the Nile in late spring would bring death to the plants and animals that depended on its water. The floods of July through October brought life back to those areas.

Civilization developed along the banks of the Nile because the agricultural society there needed to control the water and crops to survive during drought times. This was done most efficiently by people who grouped together in towns and villages. The small towns grew into trading, political, and religious centers.

THE AGE OF THE PHARAOHS

Egyptians eventually settled into a civilization made up of two kingdoms: the Red Land of Upper Egypt in the south and the Black Land of Lower Egypt along the Nile Delta. In about 3100 B.C. the ruler of Upper Egypt, King Menes, "the Founder," united the two kingdoms and became Egypt's first pharaoh. The capital was established at the city of Memphis.

Power was centralized in King Menes, who was a god-king—someone who was believed to be both a divine deity and a king. The unification of Upper and Lower Egypt was regarded by ancient Egyptians as the most important event in history, comparable to the creation of the universe. At this time the population of Egypt was estimated to have numbered about 200,000. (At the height of pharaonic Egypt, the population would grow to about 5 million.)

Menes, like all the other pharaohs, passed his powers along to family members when he died. They later passed their power down to their family members. These ruling families were called dynasties. Between 3100 and 332 B.C., Egypt was ruled by thirty such dynasties.

With the unification of the two lands under Menes, the glorious age of pharaohs began. Power was centralized and all of the growing country's economic, political, and religious institutions fell under royal authority. The central government employed soldiers, scholars, servants, bureaucrats, and artisans whose goods and services were used to benefit the upper classes and nobility. These workers also developed a sophisticated tradition of art and learning that established a long pattern of Egyptian civilization.

The pharaonic system enabled the ancient Egyptians to lead the world in innovation and invention. Even before Menes united the two lands, Egyptians had developed a type of plow and a system of writing. Egyptians were also the first to build in stone and to fashion arches with stone and brick.

Between 3100 and 2686 B.C.—periods known as the First Dynasty and the Second Dynasty—Egyptians became accomplished shipbuilders and sailors. They charted the stars and planets in the heavens and thus were able to predict the annual flood of the Nile. This led them to develop the concept of the year and the twelve monthly divisions of the calendar.

Egyptians developed the plow and a system of writing, and were the first people to build in stone and fashion arches out of stone and brick.

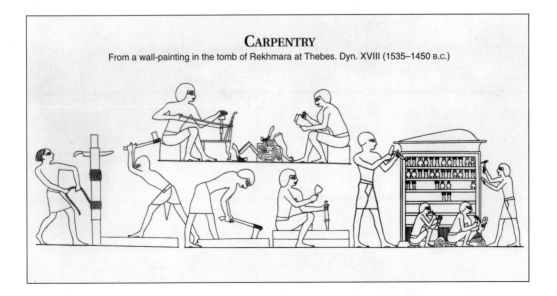

CARPENTRY
From a wall-painting in the tomb of Rekhmara at Thebes. Dyn. XVIII (1535–1450 B.C.)

HIEROGLYPHS

As early as 3000 B.C., Egyptians were writing with picture symbols called hieroglyphs (Greek for "sacred writings"). By 300 B.C. the Egyptian alphabet consisted of more than seven hundred hieroglyphic symbols. Hieroglyphs were carved into stone monuments to detail the life of the nobles buried therein. The letters were also written in ink on papyrus scrolls. (Egyptians used the fibers of the papyrus plant to make paper.)

Some hieroglyphs obviously represented objects—two wavy lines meant water, a bird symbol was a bird. But hieroglyphs could also stand for ideas. For instance, walking feet meant the passage of time.

Some hieroglyphs represented words that sound alike but have different meanings, called homophones. Thus, the pharaoh named Narmer (known as King Menes) had his name written with a fish (n'r) and a chisel (mr). Other symbols stood for sounds or designated a word as singular, plural, noun, or verb.

The meaning of Egypt's hieroglyphs was lost for thousands of years. Even native Egyptians could not read the mysterious inscriptions carved into the stone walls of tombs and pyramids. This all changed when French conqueror Napoléon Bonaparte landed in Egypt in 1798 with his army and fifty scholars. The French discovered a large stone called the Rosetta Stone, on which examples of hieroglyphs and also Greek writing appeared.

In 1822, after spending ten years studying the Rosetta Stone, French professor Jean-François Champollion became the first person in modern times to decipher hieroglyphs. After that, scholars have been able to interpret ancient Egyptian writing.

Egyptians wrote with picture symbols called hieroglyphs.

Egyptian doctors prescribed herbs and other substances as healing remedies, and they performed surgical operations. Egyptian artisans sculpted in stone and painted tomb murals with vibrant colors. And Egyptians left exhaustive records of their accomplishments carved in stone across the pyramids and tombs that scholars still study today.

THE OLD AND MIDDLE KINGDOMS

Kingdom is the term historians have given to the periods of ancient Egyptian history in which the central government was strong, the country was unified, and there was an orderly succession of pharaohs. At other times, however, authority broke down, civil wars broke out, or the country was occupied by foreigners. These periods were known as the "intermediate periods."

The Old Kingdom (2575–2134 B.C.) and the Middle Kingdom (2040–1640 B.C.) are believed to be the most important phases of ancient Egyptian history. During these periods the political and economic system of Egypt developed around the divine god-king who was believed to control the Nile through his magical powers for the good of Egypt. The cult of the pharaoh was given monumental expression through great religious complexes centered in and around the pyramids.

The pharaoh ruled by decree, which was believed to be handed down from the gods. In the early years the pharaoh's sons and close relatives acted as his aides and advisers. Other officials under the pharaoh included administrators, scribes, priests, and nobles. Merchants made up the middle-class while farmers, herders, artisans,

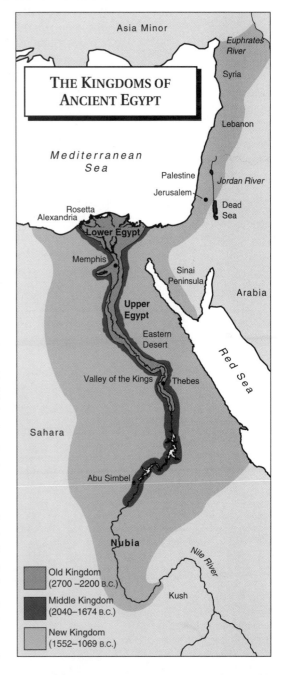

THE KINGDOMS OF ANCIENT EGYPT

Asia Minor
Euphrates River
Syria
Lebanon
Mediterranean Sea
Palestine
Jordan River
Jerusalem
Rosetta
Alexandria
Dead Sea
Lower Egypt
Memphis
Sinai Peninsula
Arabia
Upper Egypt
Eastern Desert
Red Sea
Valley of the Kings
Thebes
Sahara
Abu Simbel
Nubia
Nile River
Old Kingdom (2700–2200 B.C.)
Middle Kingdom (2040–1674 B.C.)
Kush
New Kingdom (1552–1069 B.C.)

fishermen, boatbuilders, and homemakers made up the working class. By the Fourth Dynasty, there was also a chief minister, called a grand vizier, who was a prince of royal blood and sat at the head of every government department.

Egypt was divided into nomes, or districts. Each was overseen by a *nomarch*, or governor. The post of *nomarch* became hereditary, and governors passed the job down to their sons. These men acquired large parcels of tax-exempt land. From the middle of the Fifth Dynasty, these powerful lords ruled over thousands of less fortunate subservient farmers, called serfs.

The Old Kingdom ended when the central government collapsed during a period of low Nile waters and great famine. In the absence of a strong central government, the hereditary landowners took control and maintained order in their own areas. Their estates turned into miniature kingdoms. This period of decentralized rule lasted from the Seventh through Eleventh Dynasties.

The kings of the Twelfth Dynasty restored central government and a strong kingship. This period was known as the Middle Kingdom. The Middle Kingdom ended in about 1640 B.C., when Egypt was conquered by the Hyksos—a Semitic tribe of nomads. The Hyksos are remembered for little more than having introduced the horse-drawn chariot to Egypt.

The Hyksos, who conquered Egypt in 1640 B.C., are remembered for introducing the horse-drawn chariot.

GODS AND GODDESSES IN ANCIENT EGYPT

Egyptians believed that life on the earth was only one part of an individual's total life. After death a person was believed to enter the afterlife for eternity. Religious and poetic incantations from the *Book of the Dead* were used to gain entrance into the afterlife.

The *Book of the Dead* is discussed in the 1914 book *The Nile* by E. A. Wallis Budge, the keeper of the Egyptian and Assyrian antiquities at the British Museum:

> The religious nature of the Egyptians includes a large number of works, of which the most important is the collection of chapters generally called the Book of the Dead; in Egyptian its name is *per em hru*, "Coming forth by day." Selections from this work were written in [hieroglyphics] upon coffins as early as . . . B.C. 2500. . . . The walls of tombs were covered with extracts from it, and scribes and people of rank had buried with them large rolls of papyrus inscribed with its principal characters, and ornamented with vignettes. . . . Some of the chapters in the work are of very great antiquity; and as far back as B.C. 3500 the text was so old that scribes could not understand it all.[4]

Egyptians believed that after death the god Osiris and forty-two judges weighed the dead person's heart on a scale, balancing it against a feather to see if it was heavy with sin. Printed below is Spell 30B from the *Book of the Dead*, in which a dead man pleads with his heart before it is weighed against the feather of righteousness:

> O my heart, which I had from my mother! O my heart, which I had from my mother! O my heart of my different ages! Do not stand up as a witness against me, do not be opposed to me in the tribunal, do not be hostile to me in the presence of the Keeper of the Balance, for you are my ka [life force] which was in my body, the protector who made my members hale. Go forth to the happy place whereto we speed; do not make my name stink to the Entourage who make men. Do not tell lies about me in the presence of the god; it is indeed well that you should hear. [5]

The Egyptians had many gods, both male and female. Each had different forms and powers. Thousands of temples were built to honor these gods, and the gods were believed to live in the temples in the form of statues. Each day, a god's shrine would be opened and his or her statue would be dressed and given offerings of food and drink.

The reigning pharaoh was believed to be the son of the sun god, Amon, also known as Re, who was represented as a male figure with a ram's head. The god of the afterlife was Osiris, who was represented as a mummy with a king's crown on his head. Anubis, or Anpu, was the god of the dead who was represented by either a black jackal or a male figure with a dog's head.

Isis was the queen of the gods and sister-wife to Osiris. Isis was represented by a female figure on a throne with a headdress. Hathor, the protector of women and the goddess of love and joy, was represented by a female figure with horns. Hathor was also said to have invented beer. The goddess of music and dance was Bast, daughter of the sun god, who was a cat or a woman with a cat's head.

The Egyptians celebrated many religious festivals, most of which centered on the annual flooding of the Nile and the life-giving power of the sun. There were festivals for birth, death, and the crowning of the pharaoh. Gods and goddesses had their own particular festivals, which were celebrated at various times of the year. Festivals featured animal sacrifice, feasting, drinking, and dancing.

An ancient temple panel depicts the Egyptian god Osiris weighing the heart of the dead on a scale to see if it is heavy with sin.

PYRAMID BUILDING IN THE OLD KINGDOM

With the beginning of the Third Dynasty in 2649 B.C., Egypt entered five centuries of high culture known as the Pyramid Age. Most pyramids were built during the Old Kingdom and are located on the west bank of the Nile in a region approximately sixty miles long and situated south of the delta, between Hawara and Abu Ruwaysh. Since the pharaohs believed they would have eternal life, they built fabulous tombs for themselves. The earliest pharaohs built mastabas, which were low, flat-topped mud-brick structures with slanting sides.

The architect Imhotep built the first pyramid, called the Step Pyramid, at Saqqara for King Djoser in about 2650 B.C. The structure, which measured 389 by 462 feet at its base and rose to a height of 204 feet, consisted of six large mastabas of diminishing size that were stacked upon one another. The steps were supposed to be a staircase that would enable Djoser to ascend to heaven after death.

The first true pyramid was built fifty years after Djoser's death on the sands of Meidum, about forty miles south of Memphis. The Meidum pyramid marked a drastic change in pyramid design. Workers packed the tomb's huge steps with rough-cut stones to create a sloping edge, then encased the entire structure in limestone to give it the smooth, continuous sides of a perfect pyramid. Egyptologists—people who study ancient Egypt—believe that the pyramid at Meidum was built for King Snefru. Snefru went on to build two more pyramids, the Bent Pyramid and the Red Pyramid.

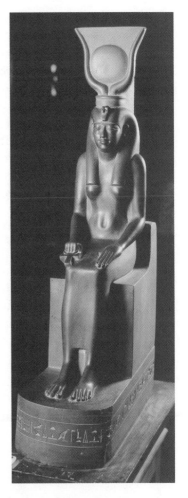

Isis, queen of the Egyptian gods, is represented by a female figure on a throne with a headdress.

Snefru's son Cheops (also known as Khufu) wanted to outdo his father, so he ordered the construction of the Great Pyramid at Giza. Cheops was a tyrant who brought Egyptian business to a halt in order to make labor available to build his pyramid. In about 450 B.C. Greek historian Herodotus wrote about Cheops and the building of the Great Pyramid:

> Cheops became king over [the Egyptians], and he drove them into the extremity of misery. For first he shut up all the temples, to debar them from [worshiping] in them, and thereafter he ordered all Egyptians to work

for himself. To some was assigned the [job of] dragging of great stones from the stone quarries in the Arabian mountains as far as the Nile; to others he gave orders, when these stones had been taken across the river in boats, to drag them, again, as far as the Libyan hills. The people worked in gangs of one hundred thousand each for a period of three months. The people were afflicted for ten years of time in building the road along which they dragged the stones—in my opinion a work as great as the pyramid itself. For the length of the road is more than half a mile, and its breadth is sixty feet, and its height, at its highest, is forty-eight feet. It is made of polished stone, and there are figures carved on it.[6]

After the death of Cheops, his son Khafre and grandson Menkure built two smaller pyramids at Giza.

The classical pyramids at Giza all contained a temple complex that was located a short distance from the pyramid and was connected by a causeway to a mortuary temple. The Great Pyramid has the most elaborate temple.

The Step Pyramid was built to aid King Djoser's ascent to heaven after death.

THE GREAT PYRAMID

The pyramids of Egypt are the world's oldest and largest stone monuments. Pharoahs from the Fourth Dynasty built the most famous pyramids—three around Giza, west of Cairo. The largest of these is the Great Pyramid, which was built to hold the body of King Cheops more than forty-five centuries ago in 2600 B.C.

Each of the four sides of the Great Pyramid measures 756 feet (one seventh of a mile) at the base. The entire pyramid covers 13 acres, or 7 city blocks. This mountain of stone consists of more than 2.3 million stones that weigh an average of 5,000 pounds each. The largest block weighs 30,000 pounds. The tip of the pyramid is 481 feet off the ground—higher than a 40-story skyscraper. (By comparison, the Statue of Liberty is 303 feet tall.)

The building and equipping of funerary sites such as the Great Pyramid represented the largest industry of the Old and Middle Kingdoms. Vast amounts of Egypt's resources were channeled into building these tombs.

Likewise, Egyptian kings filled their pyramids with riches, food, furniture, and pets, all to assist them in the afterlife. Builders of the pyramids constructed mazes of shafts, passageways, galleries, chapels, courts, and other rooms for rituals connected with the king's afterlife.

The magnificent Great Pyramid of Giza.

The Egyptians also built a guard to stand permanent watch over Giza—the Great Sphinx. King Khafre ordered the colossal statue, which is 240 feet long and 66 feet high at its head. It was carved from the ragged outcrops left behind at a quarry site where pyramid rocks were mined. The statue has Khafre's face, complete with his royal headdress and traditional false beard. The body is that of a reclining lion, the mythical creature Egyptians believed guarded sacred sites. For most of its forty-five centuries, the Great Sphinx was

For almost forty-five centuries, the Great Sphinx lay buried up to its neck under drifting desert sand.

buried up to its neck under drifting desert sands. It has only been exposed as it is today since 1926.

Three hundred years or so after the completion of the Great Sphinx and the three pyramids at Giza, the great age of pyramid building came to an end. Pepi II was the last king to rule over a centralized government in Egypt for several centuries. He erected the final Old Kingdom pyramid at Saqqara. To recapture the glories of the past, later pharaohs revived pyramid building in the Twelfth Dynasty of the Middle Kingdom (2040–1640 B.C.). However, these pyramids were smaller and made of sun-dried mud and brick rather than stone blocks. They eventually crumbled into mounds of rubble, worn down by Egypt's sun, wind, and occasional heavy rains.

Beginning in the tenth century A.D. the entire Giza complex served as a source of building materials for the construction of the city of Cairo. As a result, all three pyramids were stripped of their original smooth outer facing of limestone. The temples, like the pyramids, were mined of their rocks for the building of Cairo. They have disappeared, with the exception of the extremely well preserved granite temple of Cheops.

IN AND AROUND THE PYRAMIDS

Much of what the world has learned about the ancient Egyptians came from scholars exploring the tombs of the pharaohs. Because of the desert dryness, these burial sites containing bodies and thousands of items have remained intact throughout the centuries.

Many sites have been decimated by tomb robbers, both ancient and modern. The size and complexity of some of the burial sites, however, foiled grave robbers for centuries. In 1920, for example, archaeologist Herbert Winlock of New York found a treasure trove in an undiscovered room of the four-thousand-year-old tomb of a court bureaucrat named Meketre at Deir el-Bahri, located near the vanished city of Thebes.

Winlock found a secret chamber packed with hundreds of items that were to be used by Meketre in the afterlife. Besides food and drink, the tomb contained beds, couches, hand mirrors, perfume, and other luxury items. Meketre, like other rich and mighty Egyptians, also took servants to the tomb—not human beings, but carved figures who were believed to take care of their masters.

The Great Sphinx stands watch over Giza.

Meketre's tomb contained twenty-four little boxes that represented rooms and courtyards. They were filled with butchers, bakers, brewers, spinners, weavers, carpenters, and scribes—all laboring at their tasks. These boxes offered an intimate view of life in ancient Egypt—the baker, for instance, stood in a vat, kneading dough with his feet.

Models of boats surrounded Meketre. One portrayed Meketre and his sons, another boat carried a blind musician playing a harp, and a third boat was a floating cook's galley to provide food for the master.

THE NEW KINGDOM AND TUTANKHAMEN

In about 1550 B.C. the Egyptians routed the Hyksos, expelling them from power. This ushered in a period called the New Kingdom (1550–1150 B.C.). During the New Kingdom Egypt

MUMMIES

Ancient Egyptians preserved the bodies of their dead by making them into mummies. The word itself is derived from the Persian *mumiai,* which means "pitch" or "asphalt," and they are called this because Egyptian mummies of the late period were often coated with a layer of black resin resembling pitch.

The Egyptians placed great importance on preserving the human body because they believed that the spirit returned to it when visiting its tomb. Animals and sacred birds were also mummified and buried in special cemeteries.

Mummification was a complicated process that took as long as seventy days. The first step in mummification was to remove the brains, lungs, and lower organs—all believed by the Egyptians to be worthless. Next the body was packed in a salt called natron, which dried the tissues and kept them from breaking down. Then other internal organs were removed, with some being preserved in vessels called canopic jars and others being buried with the body. At this point embalming fluids and pastes were applied to preserve the skin and body interior. Finally the body was wrapped in many layers of linen strips with appropriate jewel-encrusted amulets (magical charms) sandwiched between the layers.

Mummies of the rich and powerful were then placed in stone coffins along with scrolls of prayer books and other instructions for navigating the mysterious world of the dead.

DIETS OF THE DEAD

Wealthy Egyptians went to the grave with everything they needed in the afterlife—including full-course meals. In a tomb near the site of the long-vanished city of Thebes, archaeologists found bowls heaped with well-preserved bread, duck, fried fish, and figs. This indicated that the diet of the ancient Egyptians was well-rounded and quite appealing.

Egyptians lived on cucumbers, beans, lentils, peas, and lettuce as well as fruits such as dates, pomegranates, and watermelon. Poor Egyptians subsisted on a plant-based diet, but wealthier ones consumed a variety of eggs, fish, fowl, beef, pork, and wine, which was carefully labeled as to year and vintage. Egyptian cooks spiced up their dishes with cumin, coriander, parsley, and fenugreek. Cakes and pastries were baked with chocolate-like carob, fruit, and honey. All of these items have been found in burial tombs.

Beer and bread made from wheat and barley were standard fare at even the poorest Egyptian burial sites. Beer was a popular drink in ancient Egypt, even with children. The builders of the pyramids were partially paid in beer. Women in every home brewed beer, and there were several large commercial breweries along the banks of the Nile. Pharaohs even received beer as payment for taxes. One record in Egypt's Middle Kingdom shows that the royal court received 130 jars of beer every day. Upon death, even the poorest Egyptian citizen was buried with a few jars of beer to supply him or her in the afterlife.

reached its peak in power, wealth, and territory. The government was organized into a military state with power centralized once again in the hands of the pharaoh and his chief ministers. Through intensive military campaigns, Palestine, Syria, and other areas were annexed by the New Kingdom.

The New Kingdom era remains one of the golden epochs in ancient Egyptian history because so much of its wealth remains. The temple of Karnak at Thebes (which still survives) grew and expanded, each pharaoh adding a room or hall, with intricately carved hieroglyphic inscriptions on every wall and pillar. Much of what is known today about ancient Egypt comes from the stories told by these inscriptions. The treasures of the tomb of Tutankhamen (who ruled from 1361–1352 B.C.) also offer modern people a glimpse into the dazzling art of that period.

The New Kingdom was marked by temple building, which began with the female pharaoh Queen Amenophis III at Thebes. Amenophis also introduced enormous statues called colossi. Amenophis's Colossi of Memnon still dominate the plain at Luxor. Ramses II was the most vigorous builder of the New Kingdom; nearly half the temples remaining in Egypt date from his reign.

Ancient Egypt entered the era known as the late period from 664–323 B.C. During these years Egyptian culture came under pressure from the Greeks and Romans in the Mediterranean and from the Persians in the Near East. As a result, the central government began to crumble. Egyptian pharaohs ruled over the Twenty-Sixth Dynasty from 664 to 525 B.C., after which Egypt became a Persian province ruled by Persian pharaohs throughout the Twenty-Seventh Dynasty (525–404 B.C.). The Twenty-Eighth through Thirtieth Dynasties (404–343 B.C.) were the last of the Egyptian pharaohs—

KING TUTANKHAMEN

Tutankhamen is one of the most famous Egyptian kings because his tomb was the richest of the few royal burial chambers that have survived intact. The pharaoh was only nine years old when he succeeded his brother, and he only lived to be nineteen.

All the other tombs in the Valley of the Kings were plundered, but Tutankhamen's was hidden by rock chips that were dumped nearby after cutting the tomb of a later king. In 1922 Howard Carter discovered the four-room tomb, which was jam-packed with three thousand extraordinary treasures, including a solid-gold coffin, a gold mask, an ivory-and-gold-encrusted throne, and gold jewelry.

Tutankhamen was entombed with a dizzying array of furniture, including three couches carved into animal shapes, chests, chairs, and stools. For sport in the afterlife, Tutankhamen had a chariot, 130 walking sticks, 46 bows, 400 arrows, clubs, boomerangs, and knives. To clothe himself in the afterlife, King Tut was equipped with sandals, necklaces, mirrors, slippers decorated with gold, linen loincloths, and 27 pairs of embroidered gloves. In the way of food, Tutankhamen was buried with 11 baskets of watermelon seeds and 30 large jars of vintage wine.

and also the last Egyptians who would rule over Egypt until the twentieth century.

In 333 B.C. Greek conqueror Alexander the Great drove out the Persians, and the great age of ancient Egypt was swept aside with the drifting sands of the desert.

The temple at Karnak stands as a symbol of the temple building done during the New Kingdom.

3

EGYPT UNDER FOREIGN RULE

The rule of the great pharaohs ended in Egypt when the Persians took over the country around 525 B.C. For the next several centuries government and social order in Egypt went into serious decline as the country was invaded by a series of outsiders that included Libyans, Ethiopians, Assyrians, and the Persians once again.

As the power, culture, and religion of the pharaohs and their people faded into history, Egypt fell under more than two thousand years of rule by outsiders. Because of the country's strategic location, the Nile's abundant supply of grain, and the tax dollars provided by its people, Egypt would remain a prize for foreign sultans, kings, and generals until well into the twentieth century.

ALEXANDER THE GREAT

The Persian occupation of Egypt ended when Alexander the Great defeated the Persian army in November 333 B.C. Egypt was in total disarray when Alexander arrived, and the Egyptians, who suffered greatly under Persian rule, welcomed Alexander as a liberator. In 332 B.C. Alexander entered Egypt's capitol in Memphis and held ceremonies celebrating the Egyptian gods and goddesses of old. Alexander the Great was accepted as the new king of Egypt without question.

Alexander quickly established a new capital, which he named Alexandria, after himself. The city was built atop an old fishing village on the Rosetta branch of the Nile where the desert meets the sparkling waters of the Mediterranean. Alexander designed the city carefully, for he wanted to establish a naval port, a trading center, and the political and cultural center of his world empire, which eventually grew to include Greece, Egypt, the Persian Empire, and India.

THE PTOLEMAIC PERIOD

Alexander the Great died of malaria on June 10, 323 B.C. His vast empire was divided between his generals. Ptolemy, the son of one of Alexander's seven bodyguards, was made ruler of Egypt. Ptolemy founded the Ptolemaic dynasty, which endured until 30 B.C.

Under the Ptolemies, Egypt became a stable, wealthy, and influential country once again. The official language of the court, the army, and the administration was Greek. Alexandria became a world-famous Greek city whose art and architecture grew to be as impressive as that of Rome and Athens. Alexandria was a renowned center of learning and culture, attracting some of the finest scholars, artists, philosophers, and scientists in the last three centuries B.C.

Alexander the Great won the allegiance of his Egyptian subjects by celebrating the Egyptian gods and goddesses.

The Ptolemies also opened new trade routes to Greek sailors when they built a canal between the Mediterranean and the Red Sea on the site of today's Suez Canal.

Many Egyptians of the time adapted Greek speech, dress, and culture as their own. And the Greeks borrowed much from the Egyptians, particularly in religious matters. This melding of art, philosophy, and science would later influence European and Western culture for centuries.

THE RISE AND FALL OF CLEOPATRA

Despite its prosperity, Ptolemaic rule was marked by royal murders and threats from abroad. Kings and queens bickered, banished, and assassinated one another. This caused a weakness that attracted attention from rulers of the expanding Roman Empire.

The Romans supported various Ptolemaic rulers, which led to more rivalry and murder rather than peace and stability. The bloody and confusing events that led to the fall of Ptolemaic rule are some of the most famous in history. And the people involved in these plots became the subjects of countless books, plays, and movies. It all began with the seventh Ptolemaic queen, Cleopatra.

In 51 B.C. Cleopatra VII (who was born 69 B.C.) became queen of Egypt. Cleopatra and her brother Ptolemy XIII jointly ruled Egypt under Roman protection. In 48 B.C., however, Cleopatra and Ptolemy each fought for total control, plunging Egypt into a civil war. The queen lost and was temporarily banished from Egypt. Julius Caesar, the ruler of Rome, supported Cleopatra and invaded Egypt, drowning Ptolemy in the Nile. Cleopatra married another brother, Ptolemy XIV, as was the custom, but she also became Caesar's mistress and followed him to Rome, where she stayed until his assassination in 44 B.C.

Cleopatra returned to Egypt and ruled with her son by Caesar, Ptolemy XV. Cleopatra's brother Ptolemy XIV was murdered on her orders. In 41 B.C. Cleopatra formed an alliance with one of Rome's rulers, Mark Antony, whom she married in 37 B.C. The couple planned to set up a vast kingdom to be inherited by Cleopatra's sons by Caesar and Antony.

But another Roman ruler, Augustus (also known as Octavian), defeated Antony and Cleopatra in 31 B.C. Antony committed suicide while Cleopatra sought to establish a

THE LIBRARY AT ALEXANDRIA

Alexandria was famous for many of its temples and monuments, but its library, founded by Ptolemy I, contained countless masterpieces of science and literature. The library was attached to a university and research center called the Museum, after the Muses, the nine Greek goddesses of the arts and sciences.

An estimated fourteen thousand students studied physics, engineering, astronomy, medicine, philosophy, and literature at the Museum. The Royal Library next to the Museum housed tens of thousands of handwritten books and papyrus scrolls.

The Royal Library spared no effort to stock its shelves. Legions of learned scholars, assistants, and educated slaves organized, classified, and copied huge stacks of books on papyrus rolls. Although some rolls were purchased, most came from ships that docked at Alexandria's ports and were forced to surrender any works on board to the library. Later cheap copies would be returned to the hapless owners.

By the middle of the first century B.C., the number of volumes at the Royal Library numbered between three hundred thousand and five hundred thousand. All were hand-copied and most were singular volumes. Besides editions by most Greek authors, there were volumes from Indian, Persian, African, and Hebrew writers.

The library's end is one of the most tragic intellectual events in human history. In A.D. 391 the Christian emperor Theodosius I ordered much of the priceless contents of the library destroyed because he believed they were anti-Christian. In 640, when Arab legions swept through Egypt, what remained of the dusty scrolls in the library were burned to heat bathwater in Alexandria's public bathhouses because they were believed to be anti-Islamic. It would be centuries before humankind could begin to reconstruct the knowledge that was lost in Alexandria.

The library at Alexandria, which once contained countless masterpieces of science and literature, was burned because its contents were believed to be anti-Christian.

*Cleopatra,
queen of Egypt.*

relationship with Augustus. When her advances were refused, Cleopatra killed herself in 30 B.C. The former queen allowed herself to be bitten by an asp (cobra). Asps were believed to be ministers of the sun god, and their bites were thought to bestow immortality and divinity. Cleopatra's son Ptolemy XV was murdered, and the Ptolemaic dynasty ended.

The story of Cleopatra, Julius Caesar, and Mark Antony has been the subject of books and movies, including two plays by William Shakespeare—*Antony and Cleopatra* and *Julius Caesar.*

ROMAN RULE AND EARLY CHRISTIANITY

Emperor Augustus established Roman rule over Egypt in 30 B.C. Egypt once again became a province of an empire, as it had been under Persian rule. The barley, wheat, and other crops that grew along the Nile became the principal source of food for Rome. This taking of grain and other monetary wealth severely impoverished the people of Egypt.

Roman Egypt was ruled by a strong military force that guaranteed order and provided security from invasion against marauding nomadic tribes. A large bureaucracy favored citizens with Greek and Roman blood over native Egyptians, and the best land continued to be owned by royal governors. Gradually Latin, the language of Rome, replaced Greek as the language of government and culture.

It was during Roman rule that Christianity arrived in Egypt. St. Mark began preaching the gospel of Jesus Christ sometime around A.D. 37, and the church in Alexandria was founded in A.D. 40. The religion quickly spread from Alexandria to the outer regions, reaching Upper Egypt by the second century. The national Egyptian, or Coptic, church, was founded in spite of violent persecution of Christians throughout the Roman Empire.

The Roman Empire began to founder in the third century A.D. The number of Romans in Egyptian government was severely reduced by Roman civil war, famine, and other factors. By the fourth century Christianity was declared the state religion in Egypt, but the Roman Empire itself cracked in half. The eastern half, which included Egypt, was known as the

Byzantine Empire. It was ruled from the city of Constantinople (now Istanbul) in modern-day Turkey. The western half of the Roman Empire remained in Rome, Italy.

The Byzantine Empire was too weak to rule Egypt, so the country was left to Nubian and North African invaders. For the next several centuries, Egypt fought several wars with the Nubians, suffered a couple of Persian invasions, and experienced a great famine.

During this period a breach in the Christian church developed between the Egyptian Coptics and the rulers of Byzantium over the divine nature of Jesus. Coptics were killed, tortured, and exiled in an effort to force the Coptic church to accept Byzantine beliefs. By the seventh century, an extreme hatred of Byzantium had developed over the religious persecutions and the growing pressure of taxation. As a result, Egyptians offered little resistance to their next invaders.

THE ARAB CONQUEST

The Arab conquest of Egypt is perhaps the most important event in the country's history since King Menes united the two Egypts in 3100 B.C. The conquest of the country by Islamic armies forced the Christian country to convert to a Muslim one; Arabic language and culture was adopted even by those who clung to their Christian and Jewish beliefs.

The conquest was part of a joint Arab-Islamic expansion that began when the prophet Muhammad began preaching the new religion of Islam. Muhammad's teachings quickly spread, and his followers, called Muslims, waged a holy war across Arabia and into Syria and Persia.

Commander Amr ibn al-As led the Muslim army into Egypt on December 12, 639, with about four thousand men on horseback who were armed with swords and bows. The Muslims took Cairo in 641 and Alexandria in 642. In 643 the Muslim conquerors established a government and military power base at the city of Al-Fustat—present-day Old Cairo.

Egypt's new rulers treated the Copts well because they had remained neutral or supported the Arabs during the battle for Egypt. Centuries of Byzantine persecution were reversed as the Arabs gave religious and government power back to the Copts.

For the next two centuries Egypt was ruled by a succession of Islamic governors called caliphs. Each dynasty claimed to

The Islamic teachings of the prophet Muhammad won many followers.

be a direct descendant of Muhammad, and each practiced Islam in its own way. This caused rifts between different Islamic sects. The biggest split was between the Sunni and Shiite sects—a conflict that continues to this day. During this period Egypt was either ruled by leaders in the Syrian city of Damascus or by caliphs in Baghdad in present-day Iraq.

As it had for centuries, Egypt provided a rich supply of grain and tax revenue to its conquerors. In time most people accepted some form of the Muslim faith, and Arabic became the language of government, culture, and commerce. More and more Arab tribes moved in from the East, further deepening the Arab influence over Egypt.

THE FATIMIDS, SALADINS, AND MAMLUKS

In the tenth century a new dynasty, called the Fatimids, gained control of Egypt. They wanted independence from the outside rulers, who at the time resided in Baghdad. The Fatimid dynasty had ruled the North African land of Tunisia. They were Shiite Muslims who considered Muhammad's son-in-law Ali to be their spiritual leader. In 969 the Fatimid general Jawhar took control of Egypt. In 973 another Fatimid caliph built the city of Al-Qahirah (Cairo) and made it Egypt's capital. From this seat of power, the Fatimids conquered Arabia, Palestine, and Syria.

Fatimid rule ushered in a period of prosperity for Egypt. Alexandria became a major trading center for ships from

China and India. Goods from the East were traded with Italy, bringing a European influence to Egypt. Arts and literature flourished as Cairo became a center for learning.

The reign of the Fatimids would last little more than a century. As the influence of the Islamic religion spread, the Christian church became alarmed. Pope Urban II, head of the church, called on all Christians to fight in the Crusades, or holy wars, against Islam and Judaism. Christian crusaders invaded Jerusalem in Palestine and other holy places. When the crusaders marched against the Fatimids in Egypt, the Fatimid grip on the country was weakened and soon destroyed.

One of the most famous Arab warriors in history, Saladin, stepped into this breech of power. As a young man, Saladin studied the Sunni religion in Damascus. When the Fatimids asked Syrians for help against the Crusades, Saladin went to Egypt to fight. When a Fatimid caliph died in 1171, Saladin took over Egypt. Three years later, Saladin annexed Syria. As sultan of Egypt and Syria, Saladin drove the crusaders out of Palestine in 1187 and reunited the Muslim lands.

THE ASSASSINS

The English word *assassin*, which defines a politically motivated murderer, has its origins in eleventh-century Egyptian history. *Assassins* was the name given to a sect of Muslim Shiites who worked to install a Fatimid caliph in Egypt from 1094 to 1273. (During this period Egypt was mainly ruled by caliphs of the rival Sunni Muslim sect.)

The Assassins seized a string of mountain strongholds in northern Persia and Syria. From there they waged a war of terror against Sunni Muslims and Christian crusaders. They often murdered prominent officials, so *assassin* (in English) came to mean a murderer of politicians or famous people.

The word for this group actually derives from the Arabic *hashashin*, meaning "users of hashish." The drug, taken from the marijuana plant, was supposedly used to inspire Assassins to perform their terroristic work. (Although this is the word's English origin, this reference has never been proven conclusively through Arab sources.) The Assassin extremists were destroyed in Persia by the Mongols in 1256 and by the Mamluks in Syria in 1273.

Saladin, the sultan of Egypt and Syria, drove the crusaders out of Palestine and reunited the Muslim lands.

Saladin died peacefully in 1193. After his death, the lands he ruled split up into a loose empire controlled by members of his family, who were called the Ayyubids. Ayyubid rulers were surrounded by a group of soldiers and bodyguards called Mamluks, who were slaves taken from Turkey, Greece, and Asia. Mamluks were trained to be soldiers and government officials from the time they were young boys. Once their training was over, they were freed from slavery, and many went on to become very powerful in government circles.

In 1250 the Mamluks took control of Egypt. Until 1517 Mamluk sultans ruled an empire that stretched from Egypt to Syria and included the Muslim holy cities of Mecca and Medina—both in modern-day Saudi Arabia.

The Mamluks continued Egypt's traditional trading with Asia and Europe. They used their vast wealth to commission fine art and build beautiful buildings. Egypt's great cities, especially Cairo, the Mamluk capital, grew in prestige. By the fourteenth century Cairo was the religious center of the Muslim world.

The Mamluk army eventually split into competing factions and, like so many before them, lost their control of Egypt.

THE OTTOMAN EMPIRE

In 1517 a sultan named Selim I, known as Selim the Grim, conquered Egypt, defeating Mamluk forces outside of Cairo. Selim used a new weapon that confounded the Mamluks— the recently invented cannon. Selim was a sultan from the Ottoman Empire.

The Ottoman Empire was one of the largest and longest lived empires in world history. It was a Muslim Turkish state that ruled at various times over southeastern Europe and the Arab Middle East and North Africa from the fourteenth to the early twentieth century. In 1453 the Ottomans captured the Byzantine capital of Constantinople and renamed it Istanbul. Between 1512 and 1520 the Ottomans added Arab provinces to their empire.

Egypt remained under the control of the Ottomans for almost three hundred years. Ottoman caliphs ruled in Cairo, but Mamluks continued to serve as local administrators who kept order and collected taxes. During these years the Mamluk military was revived. By the seventeenth century the Mamluks had regained enough power to challenge the Ottomans. Egyptian history during this period was marked by prolonged power struggles between the Mamluks and the Ottomans.

In 1760 the Mamluks were back in control after they ousted the last Ottoman governor from Cairo. But this was a time of upheaval. Between 1784 and 1792 waves of famine and plague hit Egypt. Cairo was devastated and Egypt was impoverished by 1798, when a new conqueror appeared on the horizon.

NAPOLÉON AND THE FRENCH INVASION

Napoléon Bonaparte was the commander of the French army on July 1, 1798, when he sailed to Alexandria with thirty-five thousand men on a fleet of 350 ships. In a conflict known as the Battle of the Pyramids near Cairo, Napoléon's army easily defeated the Mamluks and took control of Egypt.

Egypt was an important country to France, as editor Louis R. Mortimer explains in his book *Egypt: A Country Study:*

Napoléon Bonaparte took control of Egypt in 1798.

> France wanted control of Egypt for two major reasons—its commercial and agricultural potential and its strategic importance to the [British]-French rivalry. During the eighteenth century, the principal share of European trade with Egypt was handled by French merchants. The French also looked to Egypt as a source of grain and raw materials. In strategic terms, French control of Egypt could be used to threaten British commercial interests in the region and block Britain's overland route to India.[7]

Napoléon began to reorganize the Egyptian government, but his control over Egypt was precarious. The French controlled only the Nile Delta and Cairo. Upper Egypt was still ruled by the Mamluks and Bedouins. In addition, the British and Ottoman governments were joining forces to expel Napoléon from Egypt. On August 1, 1798, British admiral Lord Nelson annihilated Napoléon's ships while they were anchored near Alexandria. When events did not go his way, Napoléon secretly left Egypt on August 22 and returned to France. He left behind a bankrupt treasury and a general to oversee the dispirited French army.

The French struggled to maintain control of Egypt, but finally on June 18, 1801, the French army was forced to surrender to a British-Ottoman invasion force. The last French soldiers had set sail from Egypt by the end of September.

Napoléon's failure in Egypt did not stop his ambitions. He went on to crown himself emperor of France in 1804 and took control of many parts of Europe in the early nineteenth century, including Germany and Austria.

The main impact of Napoléon's invasion of Egypt was to reveal to other European powers the vast strategic importance of the Middle East. This would begin decades of British-French rivalry for dominance in the region and entice Britain to exert its powers in the eastern Mediterranean.

MUHAMMAD ALI PASHA

After the French left Egypt, the victorious Ottoman army remained. Once again the competition between the Mamluks and the Ottomans was revived. By 1803 a third party had joined the power struggle in Egypt. This was an Albanian group that had come with the Ottomans to fight the French. Their leader was Muhammad Ali Pasha.

Muhammad Ali has been called the father of modern Egypt. He gained control of the country not only because of his leadership abilities but also because Egypt was slipping into anarchy. Other Egyptian leaders believed that only Ali could bring order to the country. At first the Ottomans feared Ali and tried to neutralize him by appointing him governor of a rural area. But in 1805 the Ottomans gave in to Egyptian demands and appointed Muhammad Ali ruler of all Egypt. His official position was that of khedive, or representative of the Ottoman sultan.

Ali had learned a lot from observing the British and French. He realized that Europe was far ahead of Egypt industrially and economically and desired to bring his country into the industrial age.

Muhammad Ali brought in French military experts to train the Egyptian army. He brought in investors to build factories to make textiles such as cotton, silk, and wool. Workers were drafted into factories to make sugar, indigo dye, glass, and iron. Ali brought in European scholars to open medical and engineering schools while also building a student-exchange program to train young Egyptians in European schools.

BUILDING THE SUEZ CANAL

Before he died in 1849, Muhammad Ali was stricken with Alzheimer's disease. The Ottoman government eventually turned the reigns of power over to Muhammad Ali's fourth son, Said Pasha, who ruled Egypt from 1854 to 1863. Said Pasha granted rights to a French firm to build the Suez Canal, which opened in 1869. The city on the canal, Port Said, was named after Pasha.

Muhammad Ali Pasha has been called the father of modern Egypt for his desire to bring the country into the industrial age.

Pasha's nephew Khedive Ismail (1830–1895), took control of Egypt in 1863. Ismail worked to improve Egypt's roads, schools, railroads, and factories. He built 8,330 miles of irrigation canals, 5,000 miles of telegraph lines, 300 miles of railroad lines, and 400 bridges. Towns and cities were modernized with the installation of water and gas lines, street lights, and transportation systems.

The lavish amounts of money spent on Ismail's civic improvements, however, left Egypt in debt to the amount of 1 million British pounds. In 1875 Ismail was forced to sell Egypt's shares in the company that ran the Suez Canal to Britain. With that sale Britain became the primary owner of the canal, with France as a minority shareholder. At this time India was a colony of Great Britain as well as a major trading partner, so the Suez Canal was of supreme importance to Britain for the shipping link it provided to India.

With the loss of the Suez Canal, Egypt was once again thwarted in its dreams of independence. Hopes for a modern Egypt began to fail as a result of pressures from European business interests, who—ironically—had been invited into the country by Muhammad Ali and his descendants.

FRENCH SAVANTS

When Napoléon invaded Egypt in 1798, he brought with him a company of fifty scientists and scholars, called savants, to study all aspects of ancient and modern Egypt. The savants created The Institute of Egypt to organize the data. According to the *Egyptian Handbook*, by Kathy Hansen, the savants studied Egypt's

> geography, ruins, flora and fauna, and people. Staffed with mathematicians, astronomers, engineers, physicians, chemists, zoologists, a linguist, a composer, an architect, and artists, the company included some of the finest French minds of the time.
>
> The artist Denon joined the army attempting to control Upper Egypt, and he, with the later help of many of his colleagues from the institute's headquarters in Cairo, risked their lives to draw the temples and survey the country. Squinting through eyes swollen shut by infection, they melted down bullets for lead when supplies of . . . pencils couldn't keep up with their demand. In three years, the savants covered Egypt, studying . . . the flora and fauna, the people, and the historical monuments: many lost their health and not a few their lives. But their work, published serially from 1801 [to 1825] appeared as the 20-volume *Description de l'Egypte [Description of Egypt]*, up till then the most complete study of a country ever conducted. Its publication aroused interest in Egypt's ancient past and in Islam, fueling the growing European fascination with the Middle East.

The publication of *Description de l'Egypte* became the foundation for modern research into the history, society, and economics of Egypt.

As the twentieth century dawned, Egypt was a country that had been ruled by outsiders for more than two thousand years. No one could predict what the destiny of Egypt was to become, but it would take two more generations before the country would find itself independent—for the first time since the age of the pharaohs.

CREATING AN IDENTITY

4

Even before the Arab conquest in the seventh century, Egypt's cultural and commercial identity had been focused eastward, toward Arabia and the Orient. With the influx of French, British, and Italian traders in the eighteenth century, Egypt began to once again look westward as it had during the Greek and Roman eras.

In the nineteenth century the cultural, commercial, and political foundations of modern Egypt were laid. Egypt's economy was integrated into the world capitalist system—raw materials from Egypt were sold to Europe, and European manufactured goods made their way to Egypt. But this modernization had a negative effect on a majority of Egypt's people.

Many peasants were forced off their land because of low prices paid for farm crops. They migrated to the cities where they joined the swelling ranks of under- and unemployed people. This included artisans who made baskets, pottery, rugs, and fine glass, many of whom lost their jobs because of an influx of cheaply manufactured European imports.

There was, however, a growing middle class composed of civil servants, lawyers, teachers, and technicians. A working class of transportation and building workers also emerged.

These new economic conditions in nineteenth-century Egypt led to the growth of a nonreligious, or secular, culture. New secular schools emerged that focused on European ideas and business methods. Secular education was associated with getting ahead in government jobs and manufacturing trades. The children of even the poorest Egyptians began to attend school.

FOREIGN DEBT AND FOREIGN CONTROL

Khedive Ismail, Egypt's ruler from 1863 to 1879, brought Egypt into the modern era by spending lavishly on civic improvements such as canals, railroads, and street lighting. But this left the country deep in debt. So deep, in fact, that Ismail asked the British and French to help Egypt with financial reform. The Europeans responded by setting up a special department, called the Caisse de la Dette Publique (Bank Office of the Public Debt), to ensure that Egypt repaid its outstanding debts to foreign banks.

By 1877 more than 60 percent of all Egyptian revenue was going to this credit department. By 1878 this European bureaucracy had taken over cabinet positions and grown more powerful than the Egyptian government itself.

Egyptian politicians, army officials, and the public resented this foreign control of their country. Ismail agreed with his own people and resisted orders from the Europeans who were dominating the Egyptian government. France and Britain decided Ismail had to be removed from office, and the khedive was soon exiled to Naples, Italy. A new leader was appointed, Ismail's son Tawfiq, who was more pliable in the hands of the foreigners. In July 1880 British, French, Austrian, and Italian officials continued to take 50 percent of Egypt's total revenues to service the country's foreign debt.

The interference of the Europeans inspired a nationalistic movement among Egypt's landowners, merchants, and army officers. The group took on the name Al Hizb al Watani al Ahli, or the National Popular Party. This group, backed by powerful army officers, alarmed the Europeans, especially the British and French who wanted to remain in control of the Suez Canal.

In 1882, to protect their interests, the British navy assembled off the coast of Egypt. Meanwhile anti-European riots broke out in Alexandria with considerable loss on both sides. To retain control of the country, the British fleet bombed the beautiful, ancient city of Alexandria in July 1882. Author Timothy Mitchell describes the aftermath in his book *Colonising Egypt:*

> Within two days most of Alexandria was turned to rubble and ash. How far its destruction was due to the British bombardment and how far to the local inhabitants who responded by setting fire to European property was never determined. . . . Following the bombardment the marines were sent ashore, accompanied by a new kind of armament invented in the 1860s, the Gatling machine gun. With the help of this rapid-fire weapon, after a week of street fighting they took possession of the town.

Machine guns then accompanied the British as they proceeded with their larger purpose, to overthrow the new nationalist government. Junior officers in the Egyptian army had assumed power a year before—promising, if not a revolution, at least an end to the absolute power of the [Turkish-Ottoman] elite and their European creditors, and to the crippling indebtedness of the peasants. They were defeated by the British forces within the space of eight weeks. In the final battle at Tell al-Kabir the new machine guns, "gave most effective support, firing with great judgment upon the enemy whenever exposed to them" [according to the War Office in London].[8]

Egypt became part of the British Empire after twenty thousand British marines took control in 1882. Although Khedive Tawfiq was the face of the government, the real power in the country was the British consul general, backed by British

The British presence in Egypt lasted long after the bombing of the ancient city of Alexandria.

troops. Immediately after taking control Britain announced its plan to withdraw its troops as soon as power was restored to the khedive. But it soon became obvious that the British presence would remain in Egypt for some time.

THE 1919 REVOLUTION

Egypt was ruled by three British consul generals until October 29, 1914. At that time World War I broke out with countries such as Britain, France, and the United States fighting Germany, Austria, and others. The Turkish-Ottoman forces joined with the Germans in an attack on the Suez Canal. Britain declared that Egypt was a protectorate (under its protection) and severed all Egyptian ties with the Ottoman Empire. Although Great Britain claimed it was protecting Egypt, its main concern was the Suez Canal. Martial law was proclaimed throughout Egypt.

In 1918, after Britain triumphed in World War I, Egyptian nationalists once again began to press for independence. That year Egyptian nationalists formed the Wafd, a delegation to voice its demands. Shortly thereafter the Wafd demanded complete independence while agreeing to let the

Egyptian women demonstrate against British occupation in 1919, marking their entry into Egyptian public life.

British control the Suez Canal. The Wafd also asked permission to go to London to make their case before the British government. The British refused their demands and sent the delegation's leaders to prison.

This sparked an uprising in March and April 1919 in which a majority of Egyptians participated. Demonstrations escalated into massive strikes by students, government officials, professionals, and transport workers. There were violent clashes in Cairo and in the cities of Lower Egypt. Railroad and telegraph lines were cut, taxi drivers refused to drive, and lawyers failed to appear in court. On March 15 more than ten thousand people marched on the palace occupied by the khedive.

On March 16 about three hundred upper-class Egyptian women in veils staged demonstrations against British occupation, an event that marked the entrance of women into modern Egyptian public life. Poorer women demonstrated in the streets next to men, and in rural areas women helped cut rail lines. The women assumed key roles in the movement when male leaders were arrested. They circulated petitions and organized strikes and boycotts of British goods.

By the summer of 1919 more than eight hundred Egyptians had been killed as well as thirty-one Europeans and twenty-nine British soldiers. Strikes and demonstrations continued for many months as the British began negotiating with the Wafd for Egyptian autonomy. On February 28, 1922, the British granted Egypt nominal independence.

Egyptian sultan Ahmad Fuad was crowned King Fuad I, and his son Farouk was named as his heir. On April 19 a new constitution was approved, and a law was issued that began a new phase in Egypt's political progress—Egyptians could now elect officials to a governing body based on Britain's Parliament.

THE ERA OF ELECTIONS AND POLITICS

Although Egypt was allowed to govern itself, the British army continued to occupy the country. According to editor Louis R. Mortimer in *Egypt: A Country Study*,

Political life in Egypt during this period has been described as basically triangular, consisting of the king, the Wafd, and the British. The basis of British power was its army of occupation as well as British officials in the administration, police, and army. The king's power rested on the rights he could exercise in accordance with the 1923 constitution and partly on the permanence of his position. The king's rights included selecting and appointing the prime minister, dismissing the cabinet, and dissolving Parliament. The Wafd's power was based on its popular support and its command of a vast majority in Parliament.

These three forces in Egyptian politics were of unequal strength. The British had overwhelming power, and if their interests were at stake, their power prevailed over the other two. The king was in a stronger position than the Wafd because his power was difficult to curb while the Wafd could easily be removed from power. The Wafd embodied parliamentary democracy in Egypt; thus, by its very existence, it constituted a threat to both the king and the British.[9]

For the next thirty years, the British, the Egyptian king, and the Wafd struggled for power and influence.

When World War II began in 1939, Egypt was once again vital to Britain's defense. Britain had to maintain Egyptian support for its military and political policies during the conflict. Many Egyptians sided with the Germans, however, not because they supported the Nazi beliefs but simply because the Germans were fighting against the British. The German support of some Egyptians severely splintered Egypt's government.

During the conflict the British parked army tanks around the king's palace as a show of force. They made King Farouk appoint a pro-British government in Egypt's parliament, which the king picked from sympathetic members of the Wafd. The Egyptians saw the king's submission to British will as a betrayal of their independence. As a result, the king and the Wafd lost much of their popularity. By the end of the war, the Wafd had fallen from power and splintered into several competing groups.

The end of the war saw the beginning of a new kind of global war—the Cold War, which pitted the Communist governments of the Soviet Union (and later China) against the democratic-capitalist governments of Western Europe and

EGYPT IN WORLD WAR II

When World War II broke out in 1939, the Allies, England, France, the Soviet Union, and later the United States, went into battle against the Axis powers, primarily Germany and Italy. For its part, Egypt considered the war to be a European conflict and hoped to avoid being drawn into it. Because of the many Axis victories in the early days of the war, it looked like the Germans would win. Many Egyptians sided with the Axis countries because they believed that any enemy of Great Britain was a friend to Egypt. Meanwhile Britain worked within the Wafd to prevent an Egyptian-German alliance.

In 1942 Germany's Field Marshal Erwin Rommel, known as "the Desert Fox," landed ninety-six thousand German and Italian forces on Egypt's northwest coast. By July they were camped within seventy miles of Alexandria. As Rommel's troops advanced toward Alexandria, they were met by two hundred thousand British troops at El Alamein. After a bloody two-week battle (October 23 to November 4), the British army prevailed. Rommel was forced to retreat to Tunisia.

The battle at El Alamein was a turning point in the war. It saved the Suez Canal for the British and facilitated Allied landings in North Africa.

the United States. The Cold War was fought over economic and cultural ideologies without ever breaking into a full-scale shooting war between the West and the Soviet Union. But many small countries like Egypt became battlegrounds where the opposing systems of government (capitalism versus communism) fought for domination.

The West was concerned that the Soviet Union would try to take over Egypt for its strategic position both on the Suez Canal and near the Middle East oil fields. Egypt found itself embroiled in the Cold War against its will. In spite of this, many Egyptians continued to push for independence from both the West and the East.

CONFLICT OVER ISRAEL

In December 1945 Egyptian prime minister Mahmud Nuqrashi demanded that the British evacuate their troops from Egypt. The British refused, and once again riots and demonstrations broke out, followed by strikes. The following year the question of Egyptian rights was taken to the newly created United Nations (UN) but remained unsolved.

In May 1948 the Egyptian independence movement was strengthened by the creation of the State of Israel. The UN and the British created Israel by partitioning Palestine into an Arab state and a Jewish state. The Egyptians, like most Arabs, considered Israel a threat to Arab power and an alien state in the Arab homeland.

When Israel announced its independence in 1948, the armies of several Arab states, including Egypt, entered Palestine to take back the country for the Arabs. They were totally defeated by the Israeli army. A UN-mediated treaty followed in 1949, which left the coast of Palestine (the Gaza Strip) under Egyptian rule. Although Israel won this battle, its conflicts with Egypt would last another thirty years.

THE REVOLUTION OF 1952

The Egyptian army was poorly prepared and badly equipped when it went into battle with Israel. After the crushing defeat, the king and government took most of the blame. One of the men who had served in the war, Gamal Abdel Nasser, commanded an army unit and was wounded in the chest. Nasser was dismayed by the inefficiency and lack of preparation by the Egyptian army.

Nasser organized a secret group within the army called the Free Officers. After the war with Israel, the Free Officers planned a revolution to overthrow the government of Egypt. Meanwhile, on January 26, 1952, (a day known in Egypt as Black Saturday) various clashes between the British and Egyptians escalated into a major riot in Cairo. British property and other symbols of Western influence were attacked and burned. By the end of the day, 750 establishments valued at 50 million pounds were destroyed. Dozens of people were killed, and hundreds were wounded.

On July 23, 1952, Nasser and the Free Officers overthrew King Farouk in a bloodless coup. The king abdicated three days later, and the coup was quickly named the Revolution of 1952. The Free Officers formed a group called the Revolutionary Command Council (RCC) to govern Egypt. Egypt was renamed the Arab Republic of Egypt, and after several months Nasser became head of state. This was the first truly independent Egyptian government in two thousand years.

TURNING TO THE SOVIET UNION

In 1953 Nasser did what so many Egyptian leaders had failed to do. He negotiated the Anglo-Egyptian Agreement, which required the British to withdraw from the Suez Canal by June 1956. Nasser's popularity was enormously strengthened by the agreement.

In a move to distance Egypt from the East-West Cold War conflict, Nasser formed the Nonalignment Movement with

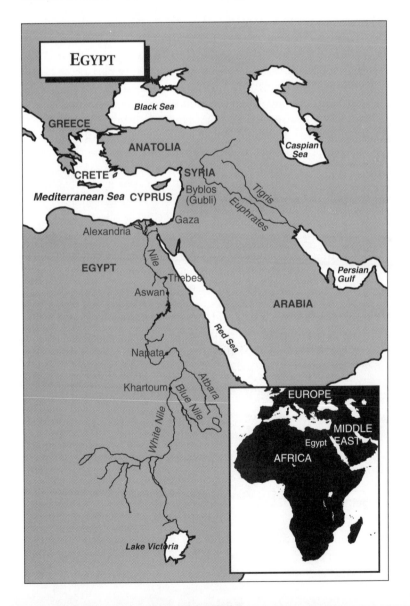

GAMAL ABDEL NASSER

Gamal Abdel Nasser led Egypt's first independent government in more than two thousand years. In the book *Egypt: A Country Study*, editor Louis R. Mortimer details the facts of Nasser's life:

> Nasser . . . came from a rural notable family. His father was from a small village in Upper Egypt and worked as a postal clerk. In 1915 the senior Nasser moved to Alexandria, where on January 15, 1918, his first son, Gamal, was born. At the age of seven, Gamal was sent to Cairo to live with his uncle and to attend school. He went to a school in Khan al Khalili, the old quarter of the city . . . where he experienced firsthand the bustling, crowded quarters of Cairo and the poverty of many in the city. Between 1933 and 1938, he attended . . . school in Cairo, where he combined studying with demonstrating against British and Egyptian politicians. In November 1935, he marched in demonstrations against the British and was wounded by a bullet fired by British troops. Identified as an agitator by the police, he was asked to leave his school. After a few months in law school, he joined the army.

> Nasser desired vehemently to change his country; he believed that the British and the British-controlled king and politicians would continue to harm the interests of the majority of the population. Nasser . . . had no particular desire for a military career, but . . . had perceived that military life offered upward mobility and a chance to participate in shaping the country's future. [Nasser wanted] to see Egypt freed of British control and a more equitable government established.

Nasser died of a heart attack on September 28, 1970.

Gamal Abdel Nasser sought to reshape his country's future.

other countries that wanted to form a third force in world politics. Through his role in the movement, Nasser became a staunch critic of the United States, Britain, and other Western countries.

When Nasser wanted to borrow money from the United States and the World Bank to build the Aswan High Dam, he was refused because of his anti-Western comments. Nasser turned to the Soviet Union for assistance and was warmly welcomed by the Communist superpower. This was the Soviet Union's first great breakthrough to undermine Western influence in the Middle East. Relations between Egypt and the Western powers reached a new low.

THE TRIPARTITE INVASION

While the Soviets started to supply money and technical expertise to build the Aswan High Dam, Nasser decided to take total control of (nationalize) the Suez Canal. The French and the British depended heavily on the canal for transporting oil supplies and felt Nasser had become a threat to their interests in the Middle East. Egypt guaranteed safe passage for all ships and promised to reimburse the Suez Canal Company for its loss. Nasser's promises were not taken seriously by the West.

After Nasser nationalized the Suez Canal, British, French, and Israeli forces invaded Egypt in what was known as the Tripartite Invasion, or the 1956 War. On October 28 Israeli troops stormed across the Sinai while British bombs destroyed Egypt's air force. French and British paratroopers dropped into Port Said and Port Fuad. The Egyptians put up fierce resistance and sank ships in the Suez Canal to prevent enemy transit, but over twenty-seven hundred Egyptians were killed or wounded in Port Said alone.

Although Egypt quickly lost to the far superior forces, the Tripartite Invasion was universally condemned by other nations. The Soviet Union threatened to launch nuclear rocket attacks on Britain and France. The United States, angered that it had not been informed of the invasion, put pressure on Britain and France to withdraw.

Faced with almost total opposition, British and French troops left Egypt by December 22, 1956. The Israelis continued to occupy the Sinai until March 1957. When they left, they instituted a scorched-earth policy, destroying roads, railroads, and military bases as they went.

Britain and France were finally out of Egypt, and the Egyptians now had full control of the Suez Canal and all its revenues. Nasser was elevated to hero status throughout the Arab world. After the Suez crisis, Nasser went on to nationalize all other British and French assets in Egypt. He also began a push to unite Arab countries to oppose Western imperialism. The Soviet Union's influence grew as work continued on the Aswan High Dam, and Soviets began selling arms to Egypt.

THE SIX-DAY WAR WITH ISRAEL

During the 1950s and the 1960s, the continued existence of Israel was strongly opposed by the Arab states. In 1964 Nasser held a series of summit meetings with a group called the Arab League, which consisted of leaders of other Arab countries, including Saudi Arabia, Syria, Lebanon, Iraq, Jordan, and Yemen. League members agreed to create the United Arab Command to coordinate military operations. The Arab League also created the Palestine Liberation Organization (PLO), whose goal was to organize Arabs who had lived in Palestine before Israel's creation to overthrow the government of Israel.

Tensions between Israel and the Arab states increased. Serious clashes between Israel and Syria occurred in 1967. Both Egypt and Syria massed troops on Israel's borders. Israel responded by deploying its own forces. With war seemingly imminent, Israel acted.

On the morning of June 5, 1967, Israeli forces launched a full-scale attack on Egypt, Jordan, and Syria. Within three hours 300 of Egypt's 430 combat aircraft were destroyed while still on the ground. Israeli ground forces initiated a lightning-fast strike into Sinai, and by June 8 they had reached the Suez Canal. By June 11, after only six days, the Arab defeat was total. Israel held all of historic Palestine, including the Old City of Jerusalem, the West Bank, and the Gaza Strip, as well as Sinai and part of the Golan Heights in Syria.

Egypt's losses in the so-called Six-Day War were enormous. Approximately ten thousand soldiers and fifteen hundred officers were killed; another five thousand soldiers were captured. Eighty percent of Egypt's military equipment was destroyed, and the Suez Canal was blocked with sunken ships and closed to shipping.

On June 9 Nasser went on television and took full responsibility for the debacle. He offered to resign, but Egypt's people poured into the streets to show their support for him. The cabinet and the People's Assembly voted not to accept Nasser's resignation.

Nasser remained in power until his death on September 28, 1970. The day he died, people once again poured into the streets to show their love and to express their grief at the loss of their heroic leader. Many Egyptians still revere Nasser as the father of Egypt, and his photo can be found in many homes and shops.

SADAT TAKES OVER

Upon Nasser's death, Vice President Anwar Sadat assumed the presidency. The war with Israel, combined with Nasser's failed policies, had severely damaged the Egyptian economy. Sadat tried to reform the Egyptian economy by initiating closer relations with the Western powers, particularly the United States. To further this goal, Sadat severed all ties with the Soviet Union in 1972 and expelled Soviet advisers.

Sadat realized that to improve Egypt's economy he had to redirect the huge financial resources that maintained the military. The best way to do that was for Egypt to appeal for peace with Israel. First, however, Sadat needed bargaining power for a basis for negotiations. To this end, he joined forces with Syria in launching a surprise attack on Israel.

On October 6, 1973, Egyptian forces poured across the Suez Canal and successfully defeated the Israeli forces stationed there. (The timing of this attack coincided with the Israeli high holiday of Yom Kippur.) Israel was unprepared for war.

After a quick infusion of weaponry from the United States, Israel was able to counterattack and succeeded in crossing to the west bank of the canal. Meanwhile the Soviet Union and the United States brokered a cease-fire agreement. After a tense several weeks, a UN emergency force arrived to administer the cease-fire. The war was over by October 24. Israel lost more than two thousand soldiers; Egypt lost eight thousand.

Neither side won a clear-cut victory. But Egypt declared victory nonetheless because it had shown that Israel, which had caused stinging Arab defeats in 1948, 1956, and 1967, was not invincible. Sadat quickly became another Egyptian

Anwar Sadat tried to reform the Egyptian economy by initiating closer relations with the United States and appealing for peace with Israel.

hero. On June 5, 1975, Egypt reopened the Suez Canal for the first time since the Six-Day War had ended eight years earlier in 1967.

CAMP DAVID

Anwar Sadat believed that Egypt needed a break from wars with Israel. In a dramatic move in 1977, Sadat flew to Jerusalem to negotiate a peace treaty with Israel's prime minister Menachem Begin. Although the war-weary Egyptians supported Sadat, other Arab nations were shocked. Negotiations remained in a stalemate for a year, until U.S. president Jimmy Carter invited Sadat and Begin to Camp David, Maryland, in the United States. On March 26, 1979, Egypt and Israel signed the Camp David Accords, which returned the Sinai Peninsula to Egypt and called for peace between Egypt and Israel.

Sadat was championed by his own country and the Western world for bringing peace to the region. But he was condemned by the Arab states, who withdrew economic aid to Egypt and voted to expel the country from the Arab League.

Most Egyptians believed the Camp David Accords promised peace and prosperity for Egypt; however, radical groups of fundamentalist Muslims were opposed to normalized relations with Israel. A member of one such group, the Islamic Jihad, assassinated Sadat on October 6, 1981, during a military parade celebrating the eighth anniversary of the war in October 1973. Sadat's assassin and four coconspirators were arrested, tried, convicted, and executed.

Hosni Mubarak, Sadat's vice president since 1974, was sworn in as president. With the peace agreement with Israel in place, Mubarak turned his attention to rooting out Egypt's corrupt government officials and rebuilding his country's industrial base.

INTO THE 1990S

Egypt continued to grow and remain at peace under the rule of President Mubarak. The country maintained its agreement with Israel and moved closer to the United States and the Western world. By the 1980s Egypt was more concerned

Anwar Sadat (left), U.S. president Jimmy Carter (center), and Israel's prime minister Menachem Begin (right) discuss the accords that brought peace between Egypt and Israel.

President Hosni Mubarak has chosen a centrist course for his nation.

about its western border with Libya than its dealings with Israel. In both 1990 and 1991, Egypt was forced to reckon with Iraq when Saddam Hussein invaded Kuwait— a move that initiated the Gulf War.

During the Gulf War, Mubarak was instrumental in forging the anti-Iraq Arab coalition that fought with the United States against the Iraqis. Egyptian troops formed the third largest allied contingent in the war. After the war Mubarak supported the regional peace process. He also backed a 1993 accord between Israel and the Palestine Liberation Organization.

As the 1990s drew to a close, Mubarak continued to follow a centrist course for his country, opposing pressures from the political right as well as the political left. While ruling with a less imposing hand than his predecessors Nasser and Sadat, Mubarak brought Egypt back into the good graces of the Arab world while continuing down the road of peace and prosperity in the Middle East.

DAILY LIFE AND CULTURE

5

Egypt has been a cultural center on the Mediterranean since the time of the pharaohs, and it has been a meeting place of East and West since the days of Alexander the Great in the fourth century B.C. Since the Revolution of 1952, Egypt has emerged as a modern Middle Eastern center of culture.

Egypt and its people have seen it all—plagues, invasions, floods, droughts, war, and peace. This "seen-it-before" attitude is expressed by three commonly used Egyptian expressions: *insha-allah* (if God wills it); *bukra* (worry about it tomorrow); and *maalesh* (never mind, it doesn't matter).

Like many other cultures, the main events of life—birth, marriage, and death—make up the most important parts of Egyptian society, along with family, friends, and food. Because daily life has changed so little for most Egyptians over the years, they tend to live in the present and worry less about the future. This attitude seems to come from a centuries-old ability to let life flow, like the Nile on its way to the sea.

ISLAM

Ninety percent of Egyptians follow the Sunni, or orthodox, branch of Islam, so Islamic religious beliefs dominate much of Egypt's daily life and culture. Islam is the state religion of Egypt as spelled out in the country's constitution.

Islam means "submission" in Arabic, and those who practice the religion submit themselves to the will of Allah. The holy book of Islam is the Koran, whose 114 chapters record the holy doctrine for the Muslims.

Prayer is very important to Muslims, and many pray five times a day—at daybreak, noon, midafternoon, sunset, and after nightfall. In cities like Cairo, tall, slender towers on mosques, called minarets, dominate the skyline. The call to prayer is given by a man called a muezzin. (Traditionally the muezzin was a blind man who would not be able to look down from the minarets into people's courtyards.) Upon hearing

the call to prayer, devout people stop whatever they are do-
ing, turn to face the city of Mecca, and bow down in prayer.

Malise Ruthven describes the Muslim call to prayer in his
book *Cairo:*

> The majority of Cairo's minarets have balconies from
> which the muezzin (crier) summons the Muslim faith-
> ful to prayer. Five times daily, from mosques all over the
> city, the call to prayer—the *adhan*—rings out, as it has
> done for 13 centuries. It is a moving and beautiful
> sound, quite different from the church bells that fulfill
> the same function in Christian countries. The muezzins
> intone the adhan in their piercing, sonorous voices—
> somewhat nasal in timbre to Western ears to a chant
> whose rhythm and melodic line are laid down by tradi-
> tion; but each muezzin selects the pitch and tempo of
> his chant without reference to the others declaiming
> within earshot. The simultaneous but uncoordinated
> sounds remind me of modern choral compositions
> I have heard in which the composer discards conven-
> tional harmony to achieve a deliberate discord. Unfor-
> tunately, the effect of this gentle cacophony is nowadays
> marred by the widespread use of loudspeakers, that all
> too often suffer seizures and blur the balanced phrases
> of the call to prayer into a continuous and deafening,
> electronic hum.[10]

*Muslim worshippers
heed the call to prayer.*

RAMADAN

The holiest Islamic holiday is Ramadan, which falls at different times of year depending on the Islamic calendar. The holiday lasts for one month; for the entire time Muslims are not allowed to eat, drink, or smoke from sunrise to sunset. During Ramadan, the streets become empty as night falls and everybody eats. Many people stay up late to eat before bedtime and get up early to eat again before dawn. The long day without food and drink is difficult for everyone.

Life changes in Egypt during Ramadan. People become very tired. Government offices will slow down or stop work completely, and it is not unusual to find people sleeping at their desks. Schools close early so students may take afternoon naps.

Not everyone fasts during Ramadan. Young children, the old and sick, and women who are menstruating are excused, along with soldiers on duty and travelers.

People follow their religion more closely during Ramadan. Families put aside time to read the Koran, and at night people gather around mosques to celebrate the end of the day's fast. At the end of Ramadan, people celebrate Eid al-Fitr. This is a national celebration, and people often travel long distances to gather with their families and break the long fast.

If women attend the mosque, they pray separately from the men. But it is far more common for women to pray at home.

Although nine out of ten Egyptians are Muslims, the 2 million Coptic Christians in Egypt are free to worship as they please. Few members of the Jewish religion remain in the country, though. What was once a large community has dwindled since most of Egypt's Jews moved to Israel after its creation in 1948. Other communities such as Protestant, Roman Catholic, and Greek Orthodox are very small and consist almost entirely of foreigners.

TRADITIONAL EGYPTIAN SOCIETY

Besides the tenets of Islam, the Egyptian character has long been shaped by traditions of the village. In the past, life in the countryside was very hard, so people were ready to help one another. This helpfulness has become a national characteristic, even in Egypt's big cities. Someone lost or in trouble today often finds him- or herself surrounded by people who want to help. Egyptians also have a strong sense of humor. Practical jokes, political humor, and jests are used to balance the hardships of everyday life.

Perhaps the single most uniting factor for Egyptians is the pride they take in their roots as people of the Nile's floodplains. Even city folks consider themselves "people of the land."

Three-fifths of Egypt's people still make their living from the land. The rural farmers who live in the Nile Valley and Delta are known as fellahin, derived from the Arabic word *falaha*, which means "to till the earth." They survive by raising crops using the ancient tools and methods of their ancestors. Most fellahin are quite poor, averaging a monthly income of less than fifty dollars.

The majority of fellahin live in small villages of one to five thousand people. Traditional houses are simple one-story buildings made from unbaked mud bricks. Today many rural houses are constructed using cement blocks. Families keep goats, chickens, sheep, and buffalo in their yards.

The lives of the fellahin seem to have changed little in the past centuries. In fact, some of the pictures of farmers painted on the walls of ancient Egyptian tombs look remarkably similar to fellahin today. But there have been improvements in medicine and health care since the 1952 revolution. Most communities have central wells that provide clean water. Electricity has also changed the lives of the fellahin. And radios and televisions have exposed many rural villagers to the outside world.

Three-fifths of Egypt's people make their living from the land.

Village people tend to live in tight-knit communities that resist change. Daily life is dominated by chores that involve tending livestock and growing crops.

URBAN EGYPT

Life in Egyptian cities differs greatly from life in rural villages. City people are able to enjoy a far more cosmopolitan lifestyle. Clothing, diet, and entertainment are often influenced by the Western world.

Cairo is a publishing center for books, magazines, and newspapers that are read throughout the entire Arab world. Likewise, Egyptian radio, television, and movie companies produce works that are seen throughout the Middle East. Western-trained physicians, architects, and other professionals use their skills to improve the lives of citizens across Egypt. But for all their Western influence, modern Egyptians retain their own cultural identity and remain dedicated to Islam.

Cairo is the heart of Egypt. Leanne Logan and the authors of the book *Egypt* describe the city of 18 to 22 million people:

> Cairo is a seething, breathing monster of a city that swallows new arrivals and consumes those who return. All are destined to be captured and captivated in some small way by its incredible past and its vibrant present. There are few, if any, cities in the world where the clash between old and new, modern and traditional, east and west is more evident. . . .
>
> No one is sure how many people have been drawn in from the countryside, even over the past few years, but the city is bursting at the seams. . . .
>
> The massive and continual increase in the number of people has overwhelmed the city. Housing shortages are rife; buses are packed to the hilt; snarled traffic paralyses life in the city; and broken pipes spew water and sewage into the streets. Everything is discoloured—buildings, buses and footpaths are brown and grey from smog and desert dust.[11]

THE LIVES OF WOMEN

Egypt is ahead of most other Arab countries in granting legal rights to women. Egyptian women are not compelled to wear traditional Muslim clothing such as veils. They can vote, own

TRADITIONAL EGYPTIAN CLOTHING

Egypt is an Islamic country, and Islamic law requires women to dress modestly. For women who are religious conservatives, this means wearing a *niqab*, which is a long dress and a veil that shows only the eyes. Some women prefer the *niqab* for the privacy it gives them in public. At home they might dress in casual wear or even trendy Western styles.

Women who dress less conservatively wear the *hijab*, which covers the body and hair but leaves the face uncovered. The *hijab* is popular because it is modest but still allows women to perform daily activities. *Hijabs* may be seen on women who are doctors, professors, and other professionals. Some younger women choose to dress in Western clothes, then switch to traditional clothing such as the *hijab* when they are older and married.

The traditional style for men is the *galabiyya*, which is a loose-fitting robe that looks something like an ankle-length nightshirt. Rural people wear the *baladi*-style robe with rounded neck and wide sleeves. *Saudi*-style is closer-fitting and buttoned up to the neck. Many men wear the traditional Arab scarf wrapped around the head while others wear the Islamic skullcap.

property, attend school, drive cars, and enjoy other rights that are only granted to men in nearby Arab nations. Compared to Western standards, however, Egyptian women seem to lead restricted lives.

Egyptian tradition expects women to raise families and look after their homes. Thus, few women reach positions of influence in government, business, or education. Government bureaucracies and government-run companies, however, are trying to change this by hiring more women. State-run television and radio stations have employed women managers, and Egypt has appointed several women as overseas ambassadors.

New attitudes do not change deeply held ideas, however. The Koran states: "Men have authority over women because God has made the one of them to excel the other, and because [men] spend their wealth to maintain [women]."[12] Therefore, to male and female Egyptians, the unequal status of the sexes is derived from the word of Allah as stated in the Koran.

In many Egyptian families, especially in the countryside, the women's position is restricted. It is almost impossible for a girl to leave home before she is married. Similarly, social customs do not allow single women to go to movies or dances without a male relative acting as an escort. Some women in rural areas never even leave their villages.

Education for women is supposed to be equal, but boys are seated in the front of the classrooms where they receive more attention. Likewise, poorer families are not likely to pay for a daughter to go on to higher education.

Egyptian women still have authority within their homes—they usually make decisions about money and legal matters. Perhaps the most important change in modern Egypt is the opportunity for women to use birth control. An increasing number of women are limiting the sizes of their families by using modern contraceptives.

Some women are concerned that they may lose the rights they have gained in recent decades. Islamic conservatives in parliament have tried to make the wearing of veils compulsory. And although it is uncommon in Egypt, Islamic law allows a man to have up to four wives. An Egyptian law that allows a woman to divorce a man who has taken another wife is under heavy fire for conflicting with Islamic beliefs.

Egyptian women traditionally raise families and look after their homes but they also benefit from many legal rights not enjoyed by women in other Arab countries.

LIVES OF CHILDREN

In the countryside children are put to work tending animals before and after school. Boys herd sheep and goats while girls milk goats and water buffalo and tend to chickens. Children also collect animals waste and form it into dung patties, which are used to fuel fires. At harvest time children work in the fields and schools do not start until the harvest is over.

If there is free time, boys will play soccer, cards, or will watch television. Girls, however, are expected to work in the kitchen with their mothers so that they learn cooking and household skills at an early age. Girls also learn how to carry loads on their heads, starting with lightweight items and moving on to clay jars filled with water.

Most Egyptians still believe that a large family is a blessing from God. In past centuries children were desired in order to help work in the fields and to look after parents when they were old. Today, as Egyptian cities teem with huge numbers of people, some couples are limiting their family size.

HEALTH

Egypt's medical system is under government control, and health care is provided to Egyptian citizens at no cost. But poor sanitation, polluted air and water, poor nutrition, and a lack of public health information make Egyptians susceptible to a wide range of illnesses. An energy-sapping disease called bilharzia is caused by small worms in the Nile's waters and afflicts about half the population. Other common diseases are dysentery, respiratory illness, and intestinal disease.

Since 1952 major improvements in clinics and hospitals have resulted in an increase in the average Egyptian's life expectancy. Since most doctors are concentrated in urban areas, the government has required medical graduates to provide health services in rural areas for at least two years.

EDUCATION

Egypt has made enormous strides in education since the 1952 revolution. Forty-eight percent of Egypt's adults can read—66 percent of men, 34 percent of women. While this is still a minority of people, it is a great improvement over earlier times.

Before 1952 education in Egypt only took place in mosques. Today the Egyptian government provides free education. Primary school attendance is mandatory. Ninety-one percent of

Egyptian children attend primary school, but half drop out by age fourteen.

Some children will go on to three years of preparatory school, followed by three years of secondary education. About 10 million students are enrolled in Egypt's twenty thousand primary and secondary schools. Secondary schools are divided into two categories: general schools and technical schools, which focus on industry and agriculture.

With a growing population and limited enrollment, competition for secondary schools is strong. Only thirteen universities exist in Egypt along with several institutes that cover the arts, including drama, ballet, and cinema. About one

Young girls learn to cook and manage a household. They can sometimes also be seen carrying loads on their heads.

hundred thousand students are enrolled in Cairo University. The one-thousand-year-old Al-Azhar University in Cairo is a major Arab center for Islamic learning.

Egypt's schools are often run-down and overcrowded. It is not unusual to find eighty to one hundred students in a classroom. Teachers are poorly paid and often must subsidize their income by tutoring. Wealthier parents often send their children to some of the few private schools available.

As in many other societies, an ongoing struggle wages between government authorities who want schools to remain nonreligious and religious purists who want religious teachings in all aspects of education.

MUSIC AND THE ARTS

Egypt has been a center of art, music, and literature for more than forty centuries, and these cultural achievements remain an important part of Egypt today. In the past 150 years, however, Egyptian painters, writers, and musicians have fallen under Western influence. Modern Egyptian artists combine Western art forms with ideas and feelings from traditional Egyptian culture. Since the Arab people had little tradition in fine arts, such as painting and sculpture, music became their main art form.

Music and dance were common entertainments for ancient Egyptians, who composed beautiful songs and hymns. Musicians played harps, six-hole flutes, lutes, and clappers. The Arab invaders brought their own instruments, including the viola, tambourine, drum, and the violin-like *rabab*.

Classical music of this period was played in mosques for religious ceremonies while the age-old chants of folk music were sung by boatmen on the Nile or farmers in their fields.

Today both classical Arab and folk music are becoming Westernized. Every village has transistor radios, and songs by superstars like Madonna and Michael Jackson are heard by millions of Egyptians.

The founder of modern Egyptian music is Sayed Darwich, who combined classical Arab music with European opera. The most famous Egyptian singer of all time was Umm Kulthum, whose music combined slow lyrical singing with traditional folk instruments. In the field of popular music, Mohammed Abd El Wahab has combined European pop with Egyptian folk music.

LITERATURE AND FILM

The Arab people do not have a tradition of writing fiction and novels, which are Western concepts. They have, however, long practiced writing poetry. Abbas Mahmud al-Aqqad (1889–1964) is considered Egypt's greatest modern poet. Even when he was jailed for political reasons, he continued to write moving poetry.

In the field of fiction, novelist Naguib Mahfouz is believed to be Egypt's greatest modern writer. His stories of life in Egypt earned him the 1988 Nobel Prize for literature and the title "inventor of the Arabic novel." In 1994 Islamic extremists tried to kill Mahfouz for using God as a character in his novel *Children of Gebalawi*.

The first Egyptian films were made before World War I, but the founding of the Misr Studios in 1934 marked the beginning of the Egyptian film industry. Many early films, such as *The Golden Chair of Tutankhamen* and *Ramses II*, focused on Egypt's ancient past. In the 1990s low-budget films and soap operas with emotional story lines are the most popular film styles. Today Cairo is known as "the Hollywood of Arabia" because of the thousands of movies produced there every year.

Attending the cinema is a popular pastime in Egypt, and movie theaters are usually full. In Cairo theaters show both Arabic and subtitled films. The most famous Egyptian film star is Michael Shalhoubi, better known by his screen name Omar Sharif.

His vibrant stories of Egyptian life earned Naguib Mahfouz the 1988 Nobel Prize for literature.

Traditional Egyptian music is closely linked with folk dancing. These dances originated to celebrate weddings, festivals, and various stages of the agricultural season. Egypt is also famous for belly dancing, which originated in Turkey.

EGYPTIAN LEISURE

The hot desert climate of Egypt and life of hard labor in the fields has helped Egyptians elevate their leisure time to what some consider to be almost an art form. In villages women gather in courtyards to talk while men spend their evenings at traditional Egyptian coffeehouses.

The typical coffeehouse is a large tiled room with sawdust on the floor. Waiters squeeze between tables carrying cups of strong dark coffee while shoeshine boys ply their trade. Men play dominoes or roll dice while they laugh and argue about events of the day. The art of conversation is well developed, and those who can entertain with wit and humor are respected. Conversations about politics and news events are sprinkled with religious quotations and proverbs. Each coffeehouse caters to a specific group of men. One may attract fellahin while another draws intellectuals or retired army officers.

Every coffeehouse has dozens of traditional water pipes, called narghiles, which are smoking devices that sit beside the tables. The brass or glass base of a narghile is filled with water, and molasses-soaked tobacco is burned over hot coals. The smoker uses a three-foot-long tube to suck the smoke through the gurgling water and into his lungs. As the smoke passes through the water, it is cooled and filtered.

EGYPTIAN FOLK ART

Although Arabic people do not have a tradition of fine art, they do have a wealth of folk art. Everyday objects are made pleasing to the eye and worthy of saving for investment. Artisans work with brass, copper, ivory, precious stones, silver, and gold. Much of the work is carried out today in the same manner as it has been for centuries.

Brass and copper objects are hammered out by hand in small family workshops. Items such as mirror frames, plates, vases, trays, coffee pots, and smoking pipes are seen in many of Cairo's shops. These items may be embossed or inlaid with stones and mother-of-pearl.

Many rural Egyptians have little knowledge of banking and invest their funds in gold and silver jewelry. This has created an entire industry that manufactures these items. Villagers prefer large, bulky designs in earrings, necklaces, and bracelets.

Regular customers at coffeehouses have their own pipes located there. Men also smoke at home, and it is the children's job to see that the father's pipe is ready when he comes home from work.

SPORTS

Egyptians love sports and most games are played there, including hockey, tennis, volleyball, handball, basketball, and squash. Soccer is the undisputed king of Egyptian sports, however. When big matches are scheduled, even the busy streets of Cairo become deserted. Those not at the stadium watch soccer on TV.

Egyptian athletes have competed in the Olympic games over the years and have excelled in wrestling, weight lifting, swimming, and track events.

FOOD

Eating is a favorite social event in Egypt, and meals involving business or family celebrations may sometimes include several courses that are drawn out for many hours.

Several vegetables play a major role in Egyptian cooking. Eggplant is used in numerous recipes and as a dip called *baba ghannooj.* Okra is widely used in soups and stews. Anthropologists believe that Egyptian olives were the first fruits to be cultivated anywhere in the world. Egyptians do not use olives for cooking but rather eat them with bread and cheese. The most common Egyptian cheese is feta, made from sheep or goat's milk. Garbanzo beans, or chickpeas, are ground up to make a dip called hummus or deep-fried in balls called falafel. Rice is a staple and is often eaten spiced with saffron.

Bread is another staple of the Egyptian diet, and people eat it at every meal. Some people eat up to three pounds of bread every day. Egyptian bread is called pita, and it is round, hollow, flat, and about the size of a dinner plate. Pita bread is cut down the middle and the hollow interior is stuffed with falafel and vegetables.

Bread is so important to the Egyptians that the government spends billions of dollars every year to offset the cost of bread for the consumers. As a result, an armful of bread only costs a few cents. The government would like to discontinue this subsidy, but when it attempted to do so in 1977, food riots broke out in Cairo.

RELIGIOUS INFLUENCE ON FOOD AND DRINK

Religion has a major influence on the foods people eat in Egypt. Pork is forbidden by the Koran, so it is only eaten by Christians. Since much of the land is not suitable for raising beef cattle, sheep and goats provide much of the meat. Camel meat is popular among the poorer people, along with pigeon, which is considered a delicacy.

According to religious beliefs, meat must be slaughtered in the proper fashion. This means cutting the windpipe and carotid arteries of the animal while quoting a prayer from the Koran that states that Allah is the creator of all things.

Alcohol is also forbidden. Under Muslim law, no Muslim is allowed to drink alcohol or to sell alcohol to a non-Muslim. This law is observed in varying degrees depending on the strength of an individual's religious convictions. Egypt has a large brewing industry, and beer, the drink of the pharaohs, may be bought openly in restaurants. During Ramadan, however, people are less likely to sell alcohol, and restaurants only sell alcohol to foreigners.

Egypt has always been at the crossroads for the world's spice traders, and Egyptian cooks use a wide variety of spices, including cumin, caraway seeds, saffron, ginger, and coriander. Some towns have large marketplaces that sell nothing but spices.

Egypt's rich and varied dishes mirror its colorful culture. By taking the best from both the East and the West, Egypt has maintained its unique and vital traditions for thousands of years.

CHALLENGES TODAY AND TOMORROW

6

Modern Egypt faces many formidable political and economic problems, which have been accelerated by changes in the past several decades. Egypt is a poor country and a crowded one. Since the mid-1980s economic hardships have forced many young men and women to leave their rural villages in search of work in Cairo and Alexandria. Poverty breeds discontent, and religious fundamentalists have tried to stanch Egypt's economic and cultural progress. However, Egypt's leaders have chosen the path of tolerance and moderation, and economic reforms are gradually making the country more prosperous and stronger.

But in regional matters, Egypt faces threats to peace on almost every side. Problems with Libya, Sudan, Israel, Iraq, and Iran continue to challenge the people of Egypt today and will, most likely, into the future.

EGYPT'S PRESIDENT

Egypt has been governed by a strong central authority since ancient times, when god-kings held absolute power over the common people. The modern Egyptian state is also rooted in the policies of strong rulers, especially Nasser, Sadat, and Mubarak—the country's three presidents since 1954.

Egypt's president is elected for a six-year period, after which he or she can serve additional terms. Nasser was president for sixteen years and Sadat for eleven—both men remained in power until they died. Egypt's current president, Mubarak, has been in power since 1981. He was elected to a second term in 1987 and a third term in 1993.

To become president a person must be nominated by two-thirds of the legislature and elected by a majority. Once this is done, the nomination is taken to the people, who must approve the president in a referendum.

Egypt's president has enormous power. He appoints and dismisses the prime minister, vice president, and his cabinet. The president defines general state policy and makes sure it is implemented. And he is the supreme commander of the armed forces. Egypt's president also controls a plethora of ministers who oversee everything from banking and tourism to the Suez Canal and the army.

THE LEGISLATURE

The Majlis ash-Sha'ab, or People's Assembly, is Egypt's law-making body. By law, at least half of the assembly's members must come from labor or farm backgrounds. Of the 454 members of the People's Assembly, 444 (2 deputies from each of Egypt's 222 districts) are elected by popular vote. The president nominates the other 10 members, who are usually representatives of the Coptic minority. Deputies on the People's Assembly are elected for six-year terms.

The People's Assembly is aided by the 264-seat Shura Council, or Consultative Assembly, which studies national issues, drafts proposals and laws, and advises the president. The Shura Council has no lawmaking power. The president appoints one-third of the members, and the others are elected by voters.

At a regional level, Egypt is divided into twenty-seven governorates (provinces). Each has a governor who is appointed by the president. Governors have considerable power and

Many rural villagers have left the country- side in search of work in Cairo and Alexandria.

GOVERNMENT CENSORSHIP

Egypt has a relatively free press, but in recent years the government has been censoring journalists for speaking out against political leaders. This problem was described in the British newsmagazine the *Economist* on March 28, 1998.

A government crackdown has cast gloom over Egypt's relatively free press. Over the past few weeks, the government has banned the most successful independent weekly and sacked the editor of a popular state-owned magazine. Three prominent muckraking journalists have received jail sentences for slander, and dozens of other writers face similar charges. The censor's hand has grown heavier; the English-language *Cairo Times* was punished for refusing to delete bits of articles. Egypt's brighter economic prospects seem, to many, to be clouded by the dimming prospects for political freedom.

Although the Egyptian government monopolises broadcasting, it exercises looser control over the printed word. Half a dozen legal opposition parties have long published their own newspapers. . . .

Given Egypt's conservative society, a legacy of censorship and the continuing menace of religious extremism, this unfamiliar exuberance was bound to get on the authorities' nerves.

make decisions about local issues, such as building hospitals and schools. Below the governor are district and village mayors with their own elected councils.

THE JUDICIAL SYSTEM

Islam is the official religion of Egypt, and Islamic law (*Shari'a*) is the guiding principle for Egyptian law. In modern Egypt, however, Islamic law is mixed with Western judicial concepts taken from France, Britain, and Italy. However, these Western concepts are considered too liberal by strict believers in Islam.

Legal questions regarding matters such as marriage and family are decided by the religious law of the people involved. Islamic people follow Islamic law while Christians, Jews, and others follow their respective faiths. The rest of

Egypt's judicial system is modeled after the French court system set up by Napoléon (Napoleonic law), which hears cases before tribunals made up of judges. There are no trials by jury in Egypt.

The Egyptian criminal code consists of three main categories of crime: contraventions (minor offenses), misdemeanors (offenses punishable by imprisonment or fines), and felonies (offenses punishable by long prison sentences or death). Lower courts handle the majority of the cases, and fines, rather than jail terms, are levied in 90 percent of the cases.

RELIGIOUS OPPOSITION TO THE GOVERNMENT

In modern Egypt the most explosive issue is the "Political Islam" movement that is campaigning to make Egypt a state governed solely by strict Islamic law. Believers in Political Islam want Islamic law to dominate Egypt's arts, education, culture, and lifestyles. Fundamentalists insist that all women in Egypt should be made to wear veils regardless of their faith.

Some Islamic fundamentalists have formed terrorist groups such as Al-Jihad (Holy War) and Jama'ah al-Islamiyah (the Islamic Group). The latter considers Sheik Omar Abdel Rahman to be its spiritual leader. (Rahman is currently serving a life sentence in the United States in connection with the 1993 bombing of the World Trade Center in New York City.)

The terrorists hope to overthrow Mubarak, and they are violently opposed to the existence of Israel and any country friendly with Israel. Various terrorist groups have killed Egyptian officials, hijacked airplanes, bombed buildings, and tried to assassinate Mubarak.

In the 1990s the Egyptian government began cracking down on terrorism. Between 1992 and 1998 the government raided terrorist hideouts in caves and sugarcane fields, jailed thousands of suspects, and tried them in military courts.

CRIME

Like many poor countries, Egypt has its share of urban petty crime, particularly theft, pickpocketing, and purse snatching. In rural areas crime victims often seek retribution and take the law into their own hands without going to the police. Most crimes in these areas occur between families and deal

Sheik Omar Abdel Rahman, the spiritual leader of Jama'ah al-Islamiyah, is currently serving a life sentence in the United States in connection with the 1993 bombing of the World Trade Center in New York City.

with issues of passion, honor, and vengeance. Bank robberies, gang activity, and other violence is uncommon.

Reliable crime statistics in Egypt are not readily available, but violent crimes not related to politics are rare in Egypt. Reliable figures from 1988 show that Egypt recorded 784 murders, 364 serious assaults, and only 14 armed robberies. These figures are a tiny percentage of similar crimes in the United States.

So-called white-collar criminal offenses are common in Egypt. These business crimes include smuggling taxed goods, embezzlement, customs evasion, trading contraband, kickbacks, black-marketing in currency, and bribes to public officials. Each year Egyptian officials arrest over one hundred

TERRORIST MURDER AT LUXOR

Although Egypt has long been troubled by radical elements of society, by the mid-1990s the Egyptian government believed it had stamped out terrorism after rounding up thousands of Islamic terrorists. This belief was shattered in September 1997, when three Islamic militants fire-bombed and then fired semiautomatic weapons into a tour bus, killing nine German tourists just outside Cairo's Egyptian Museum (considered a must-see for every foreign visitor because it houses the golden mask of King Tut).

The peace was shattered once again on November 17, 1997, when six Islamic militants posing as police officers raided the temple of Hatshepsut near Luxor, slaughtering fifty-eight foreign tourists and four Egyptians. The carnage was horrific. The killers sprayed gunfire into the throng of tourists, finished off the survivors with knives, and danced over their victims' bodies. Finally the real police arrived and killed the killers. The terrorists, who belonged to the Islamic Group, scattered leaflets claiming they wanted to replace Egypt's secular government with an Islamic regime. They also demanded the release of Omar Abdel Rahman, a sheik serving life in prison for plotting to blow up New York's World Trade Center.

The Luxor massacre caused thousands of travelers to change their plans and cut deeply into Egypt's vital $3-billion tourism industry. This was the bloodiest terrorist attack Egypt had ever witnessed. Most of the dead were from Switzerland, Germany, England, and Japan.

Egypt's many tourist attractions have been targets for terrorist groups.

thousand people for "supply violations," which include petty infringements by shopkeepers and vendors for failing to observe price controls.

The use of narcotics and other drugs has been a growing problem in Egypt. Officials estimate that as many as 2 million Egyptians use illegal drugs. Many of these users are students and the children of wealthy parents. Cocaine, heroin, opium, and hashish are the most commonly used drugs. (Hashish has been widely used by Egyptians for centuries. Opium and hashish are produced in Egypt and nearby Lebanon.) Police officials estimate that Egypt has about 250,000 heroin addicts, and the rising cost of narcotics has spiked petty crime figures when addicts steal to support their habits.

To combat this problem, Egypt has begun to impose stiff penalties on those caught with drugs, including Westerners. Penalties for smuggling and dealing drugs include twenty-five years in jail or death by hanging.

THE ECONOMY

Crime and punishment are only a small part of the Egyptian government's duties. Egyptian officials also have a strong hand in running the nation's economy on many levels from monetary policy to outright ownership of large industries. After the Revolution of 1952, Nasser nationalized many businesses and began a long period of state involvement in the economy. Sadat and Mubarak gradually reversed some of those policies.

Egypt depends heavily on foreign aid, and the Western countries that provide it have long complained that the change from a state-run economy to a free-market economy has been too slow. There have been some successes, however. Under Mubarak, billions of dollars worth of state assets have been sold to private companies, including some top hotels and factories.

One result of Nasser's socialism that remains today is Egypt's enormous government bureaucracy, which is filled with people who have little work to perform. Of a total Egyptian workforce of 15 million, about 5 million people work for the government. Since Egypt already has a chronic 20 percent unemployment rate, any attempt to streamline the bloated ranks of government employees would send the unemployment numbers soaring.

Egypt's unemployment rate was intensified by the Gulf War, when six hundred thousand Egyptians who worked in Iraq and Kuwait were forced to return home. Some workers went back to Kuwait after the war, but many jobs in Iraq were permanently lost. One positive effect of the war: Western states agreed to reduce Egypt's foreign debt by 25 percent, or $14 billion, for services rendered during the war.

AGRICULTURE

Egypt's economy is based on three main sectors: agriculture, industry, and manufacturing. Added to this are the revenues from the Suez Canal and the massive tourist industry. In addition, Egyptian workers in other countries send a significant amount of their wages back to Egypt to support their families.

Egypt's legendary Nile and the surrounding fertile lands have supported Egyptians—and a succession of foreign empires—for thousands of years. Since the 1890s Egypt has been building irrigation systems, large and small dams, and a series of canals to enable farmers to grow crops year round.

Egypt has about 6 million acres of land under cultivation, and farming provides much of the country's food needs. Cereal grains such as barley, rice, and wheat occupy over half of the acreage. Egypt's farmers also grow a wide variety of food crops such as chickpeas, lentils, vegetables, citrus fruits, nuts, and dates. Cash crops like cotton and sugarcane are used for trade to bring much-needed foreign capital into the country. Egypt produces 40 percent of all cotton grown in the world, and the crop is responsible for one-fifth of Egypt's export earnings. It also provides a base for spinning and weaving industries.

Egypt's farmers also raise cattle and water buffalo for use as draft animals, meat, and hides. Sheep are raised for wool and goats for milk. Chickens produce about 90 percent of the eggs eaten in Egypt, and pigs are raised to produce pork for foreigners and Coptics.

INDUSTRIAL PRODUCTION

Farming dominates Egypt's economy, but oil has overtaken agriculture as the major source of Egypt's foreign earnings. The oil industry employs few people, however, compared to the massive numbers who farm. There are drawbacks to relying on oil profits: The price of oil can change daily, leaving the economy vulnerable to boom and bust cycles. By producing its own oil, however, Egypt has become economically independent from its Arab neighbors.

The Romans first noticed oil oozing out of the ground near the Gulf of Suez two thousand years ago. Oil was not produced in Egypt until 1913, though, and the modern oil industry has only been developed in the past three decades. Even at the low oil prices prevalent in the 1990s, oil accounts for 55 percent of Egypt's export earnings. The oil industry is controlled by the state-owned Egyptian General Petroleum Corporation, but much of the exploration and production work is done by foreign companies who share in the profits.

Egypt's main oil fields are located offshore in the Gulf of Suez. The oil is pumped ashore, where six major refineries turn it into petroleum products. In 1990 Egypt produced about 850,000 barrels of oil per day. About half was used domestically, and after foreign companies took their share, Egypt exported about 200,000 barrels a day. It is estimated that Egypt's oil reserves will last only another twenty years or so.

Besides producing oil, Egypt has spent the last forty years developing factories such as cement plants, steel mills, textile mills, and food processing plants. Many of these factories are state run, which has resulted in poor management, overstaffing, and inefficient production. Despite its growing number of factories, Egypt still has to import a large variety of items, including food, machinery, chemicals, wood, and both paper and metal products.

THE TOURIST INDUSTRY

After oil, tourism is the second most important source of money to the Egyptian economy. Tourists have been flocking to see the pyramids since ancient Greek and Roman times. In the nineteenth century, Westerners considered it a great adventure to ride a camel out of Cairo for a full day to reach the great pyramids. Today it takes about an hour to reach the pyramids via a luxury bus.

Egypt's modern tourist industry is well developed, and cities such as Cairo and Alexandria offer travelers fine hotels and restaurants. Egypt's airlines transport tourists from the large cities to the ancient temples in the far south of the country. And modern air-conditioned coaches speed across

Tourism is the second most important source of money for Egypt, with the great pyramids as one of the biggest attractions.

the desert from one site to the next. Tourism is a desirable industry for Egypt; it employs many people and brings in vital foreign currency.

Although most visitors want to see the pyramids, Luxor, and the Museum of Egyptian Antiquities (also called the Egyptian Museum), Egypt also offers other attractions. The coral reefs in the Red Sea are popular with scuba divers, and the rugged terrain of the Sinai Peninsula is a mountain climber's paradise.

Terrorism and wars have had negative effects on the tourist industry and caused great hardship to those who depend on tourist dollars.

AN ANCIENT LAND IN THE TWENTY-FIRST CENTURY

As Egypt enters the twenty-first century, the modern world is catching up with the nation's traditional manners and customs. Crafts workers and artists are being forced from the workshops into anonymous factory production lines. Old-fashioned face-to-face business dealings are giving way to deals conducted on cell phones, fax machines, and

POLLUTION AND THE PYRAMIDS

In the past few decades Egypt's rampant population growth, industrial development, and urban sprawl have begun to threaten the country's ancient archaeological heritage. Acid rain, severe water pollution in the Nile, and unchecked construction have combined to damage some of the monuments that date back almost four thousand years.

Just fifty years ago residents of Cairo could view the pyramids, which stood some five miles away. Today only a forest of buildings can be seen between Cairo and the ancient tombs. These newly developed areas are marred by traffic congestion, a lack of running water for the residents, and no zoning or town planning.

The pyramids are not the only remains threatened by urbanization. Luxor, one of the world's most prestigious historic cities, is also under siege. It could be said that this area is being "loved to death" by the large numbers of tourists who come to enjoy Luxor's wonders.

More than 230 cruise ships ply the Nile at any one time, and the government is in the process of building a docking area so the tourists can better enjoy the view. This means that electricity, water stations, telephones, and sewage pumping systems will be required to supply boat needs. Such an infrastructure will make the area an attractive place to build hotels and restaurants and provide a good opportunity for locals to set up small businesses.

Egypt is aware of the pollution problems it faces and has implemented dozens of government agencies to monitor noise, air, water, and solid waste pollution. But as the country's population continues to grow, and as millions of tourists pour into formerly isolated regions, it is hard to predict what effects the pollution will have on Egypt's ancient treasures.

Over 230 cruise ships sail the Nile at any given time.

computers. Donkeys, horses, and camels are forced off the street to make way for motorcycles, cars, and trucks. The glory of the pyramids and the tomb of King Tut are a mere mouse-click away for users of the Internet.

Modernization will bring many long-term benefits to the poor people of Egypt. But the advancements might come at the expense of the slow-paced traditions that have developed in this ancient land over the past sixty centuries. Perhaps this idea is best summed up by the words of author Malise Ruthven in the book *Cairo:*

> I believe [modernization] would be a great shame if this new order were to be achieved at the expense of [Cairo's] most valuable resource—the humane, intimate quality of its social fabric. For, although Cairo is at present struggling to cope with a massive explosion of population, I sense that among its teeming streets human relationships remain more highly prized than they are within cities where a more streamlined—but more neurotic—lifestyle prevails. The warmth and good humour of the Cairenes are priceless assets that have served them well in the past; I feel sure that they will sustain them through whatever changes the future may bring.[13]

FACTS ABOUT EGYPT

GOVERNMENT

Full name: Arab Republic of Egypt (Misr, in Arabic)

Type: A republic headed by a president

National flag: Three horizontal bands of red, white, and black with the central white band showing the crest of Saladin, the national emblem. The emblem is a golden hawk and shield with a scroll underneath. Red, white, and black are the traditional colors for Arabic people. Black stands for Egypt's history before it was a republic, white for Egypt's peaceful revolution in 1952, and red for the passionate spirit of Egypt's people.

Year of founding: Menes, the first pharaoh, united Egypt around 3100 B.C. In 1922 Egypt became an independent nation. After a bloodless coup on July 23, 1952, Egypt became a republic under Gamal Abdel Nasser in 1953.

Legislature: People's Assembly

Government leader (1998): President Hosni Mubarak

Political subdivisions: 27 governorates

National anthem: "*Beladi, Beladi*" ("My Country, My Country")

Official religion: Islam

PUBLIC HOLIDAYS

January 1	New Year's Day
April 25	Sinai Liberation Day
May 1	May Day
July 23	Revolution Day
October 6	National Day

ISLAMIC RELIGIOUS HOLIDAYS

Because the Islamic calendar is eleven days shorter than the Western calendar, Islamic holidays fall in different months in different years. These are the major Islamic holidays:

Moulid an-Nabi	Birthday of the prophet Muhammad
Ramadan	The month over which the Koran was revealed to Muhammad; Muslims celebrate this event by fasting from dawn to dusk.
Eid al-Fitr	The end of Ramadan; feasting and celebration lasts for three days.
Eid al-Adha	The time when Muslims make pilgrimages to Mecca

PEOPLE

Population (1995): 61.9 million

Annual growth (1995): 2.3 percent or 1.4 million per year

Distribution (1995): 44 percent urban; 56 percent rural

Overall population density: 160 persons per square mile (62 persons per sq km)

Life expectancy at birth (1995): female, 65 years; male, 62 years

Infant mortality (1995): 62 deaths per 1,000 live births

Major cities: Cairo, Alexandria, Giza, Shourbra al-Kheima, Port Said

Major religions: Islam (90 percent Sunni Muslim); Coptic Christianity

Official language: Arabic, with some French and English

Education: About 91 percent of Egyptian children attend primary school, but half drop out by age fourteen. About 10 million students are enrolled in Egypt's 20,000 primary and secondary schools.

Literacy (1990): Forty-eight percent of Egypt's adults can read—66 percent of men, 34 percent of women.

GEOGRAPHY

Area: 386,661 square miles (1,001,449 sq km)

Capital and largest city: Cairo (1994 est. pop., 6.85 million; Greater Cairo has a population of at least 15 million)

Highest point: Gebel Katherina (Mount Saint Catherine), 8,651 feet (2,637 m)

Lowest region: Qattara Depression, 436 feet (133 m) below sea level

Coastline: Egypt extends along the Mediterranean Sea for approximately 450 miles (760 km). The Red Sea borders Egypt's east coast for about 450 miles (760 km) and is connected to the Mediterranean by the Suez Canal.

Major rivers: The Nile extends through Egypt for about 950 miles (1,605 km).

Deserts: Ninety-six percent of Egypt is desert, and its two largest land regions are the Eastern Desert and the Western Desert, which is part of the Sahara Desert.

Lakes: Lake Nasser, at 312 miles (527 km) long, is the largest artificial lake in the world. It was formed when the Nile River was dammed by the Aswan High Dam.

CLIMATE

| | JULY | | JANUARY | |
	°C	°F	°C	°F
Alexandria	30/23	86/73	19/10	66/51
Cairo	35/21	96/71	19/07	66/45
Luxor	41/22	107/72	23/05	74/42
Aswan	41/25	107/78	24/09	75/49

Annual rainfall: Egypt is a desert and gets very little rainfall. Aswan receives less than 0.1 inch (0.0025 m) and some parts of the desert have not received rain in 20 years.

ECONOMY

Monetary unit: Egyptian pound, equal to 100 piastres

(All following monetary figures are in U.S. dollars)

Gross national product (1993): $36.7 billion. Agriculture contributes 43 percent to the economy; mining and manufacturing—16 percent; construction—6 percent; trade and finance—15 percent; public administration, defense, and services—20 percent.

Annual per capita income (1993): $660

Unemployment rate: 20 percent plus

Exports: Approximately $3.6 billion a year. Main exports are cotton, sugar, tobacco, and petroleum.

Imports: Approximately $10 billion. Main imports are food, machinery, chemicals, wood, and paper and metal products.

Major trading partners: United States, Italy, Germany, France, Israel

ARMED FORCES

In 1990 Egypt had approximately 450,000 people in the armed forces. Forces consisted of 320,000 in the army; 20,000 in the navy, including 2,000 in the coast guard; 30,000 in the air force; and air defense forces, a separate service of 80,000.

Egypt also has an internal security force of about 120,000 members of the national police force and 300,000 members of the central security forces, who guard buildings and control demonstrations. The General Directorate for State Security Investigations has a classified number of members who monitor suspected subversive and extremist groups.

NOTES

INTRODUCTION: EGYPT: CROSSROADS OF THE WORLD

1. Quoted in Ann Heinrichs, *Egypt*. New York: Childrens Press, 1997, p. 11.

CHAPTER 1: GEOGRAPHY AND POPULATION

2. Quoted in Heinrichs, *Egypt*, p. 93.
3. Edward William Lane, *An Account of the Manners and Customs of the Modern Egyptians*. New York: Dover, 1973, pp. 288–89.

CHAPTER 2: ANCIENT HISTORY

4. E. A. Wallis Budge, *The Nile*. London: Thomas Cook & Son, 1912, p. 303.
5. Quoted in R. O. Faulkner, trans., *The Ancient Egyptian Book of the Dead*. New York: Macmillan, 1985, pp. 27–28.
6. Herodotus, *History*. Chicago: University of Chicago Press, 1987, p. 185.

CHAPTER 3: EGYPT UNDER FOREIGN RULE

7. Louis R. Mortimer, ed., *Egypt: A Country Study*. Washington, DC: Library of Congress, 1991, p. 27.

CHAPTER 4: CREATING AN IDENTITY

8. Timothy Mitchell, *Colonising Egypt*. Cambridge: Cambridge University Press, 1988, p. 128.
9. Mortimer, *Egypt: A Country Study*, p. 49.

CHAPTER 5: DAILY LIFE AND CULTURE

10. Malise Ruthven, *Cairo*. Amsterdam: Time-Life International, 1980, p. 71.
11. Leanne Logan et al., *Egypt*. Hawthorn, Australia: Lonely Planet, 1996, p. 135.
12. Quoted in Ruthven, *Cairo*, p. 143.

CHAPTER 6: CHALLENGES TODAY AND TOMORROW

13. Ruthven, *Cairo*, p. 197.

CHRONOLOGY

B.C.
3100
King Menes unites Upper and Lower Egypt and becomes the first pharaoh of the kingdom of Egypt.

2500
Egyptians build the pyramids and Great Sphinx at Giza.

1600s
The Hyksos rise to power, ending the pharaonic reign of the pyramid builders of Egypt's Middle Kingdom.

1500s
The Hyksos are driven out, and Thebes becomes the capital of Egypt.

1300s
King Tutankhamen reigns until his death at about age nineteen.

664–525
The last great pharaohs rule over Egypt, after which the country becomes a Persian province.

332
Alexander the Great invades Egypt.

A.D.
639–642
Muslim Arab armies conquer Egypt.

969–1171
The Fatimid dynasty rules Egypt.

1250
The Mamluks take control of Egypt.

1517
Ottoman Turks invade Egypt and rule for almost three hundred years.

1798
Napoléon conquers Egypt.

1869
The Suez Canal is completed.

1882
Britain occupies Egypt.

1914
Britain declares Egypt a protectorate.

1922
Britain grants Egypt nominal independence.

1952
King Farouk is dethroned.

1953
Egypt is declared a republic.

1956
Gamal Abdel Nasser is elected president and nationalizes the Suez Canal.

1967
Egypt loses to Israel in the Six-Day War; Israel occupies the Sinai Peninsula.

1970
Nasser dies of a heart attack. His vice president, Anwar Sadat, becomes president of Egypt.

1973
Egypt and Israel fight the October War.

1978
Sadat and Menachem Begin of Israel sign the Camp David Accords, establishing peace between the two countries.

1981
Sadat is assassinated by Islamic extremists; Hosni Mubarak becomes president.

1990
Egypt emerges as a Middle East leader after the Iraqi invasion of Kuwait.

1993

Mubarak is elected to a third presidential term; Mubarak and the Egyptian government back an accord between Israel and the Palestine Liberation Organization which is instrumental in reducing hostilities in Israel.

1994

Islamic extremists try to kill Egypt's great modern writer, Naguib Mahfouz, for his use of God as a character in the novel, *Children of Gebalawi.*

1997

In September, three Islamic militants fire-bomb then fire semiautomatic weapons into a tour bus, killing nine German tourists outside Cairo's Egyptian Museum; on November 17, six Islamic militants posing as police raid the Temple of Hatshepsut near Luxor and slaughter fifty-eight foreign tourists and four Egyptians.

1998

Mubarak takes part in talks aimed at furthering progress in the stalled Israeli-Palestinian peace process.

SUGGESTIONS FOR FURTHER READING

Peter A. Clayton and Martin J. Price, *The Seven Wonders of the Ancient World.* New York: Dorset , 1989. A fascinating book about the monuments, lighthouses, gardens, and other wonders of the ancient world, with a long chapter about the Great Pyramid at Giza.

Editors of Time-Life Books, *Egypt: Land of the Pharaohs.* Alexandria, VA: Time-Life Books, 1992. A big, beautiful book from the Time-Life Lost Civilizations series. The informative text is accompanied by hundreds of high-quality photographs and drawings of ancient Egyptian tombs, monuments, pyramids, and artifacts.

———, *What Life Was Like on the Banks of the Nile.* Alexandria, VA: Time-Life Books, 1997. Another gorgeously detailed book by Time-Life. It is illustrated with photos of statues and hieroglyphics that show the average person's work, worries, birth, death, and lifestyles in ancient Egypt.

R. O. Faulkner, trans., *The Ancient Egyptian Book of the Dead.* New York: Macmillan, 1985. A mesmerizing book that transcends centuries with 181 spells from the *Book of the Dead,* translated into English and illustrated with photos of papyrus scrolls from which the spells were taken.

Ann Gaines, *Herodotus and the Explorers of the Classical Age.* New York: Chelsea House, 1994. A book for young adults about Herodotus, which features his history essays and details the state of the world at the time they were written.

Ann Heinrichs, *Egypt.* New York: Childrens Press, 1997. A book for young adults that covers Egypt's geography, economy, language, lifestyle, and more.

David Macaulay, *Pyramid.* Boston: Houghton Mifflin, 1975. Architect and artist David Macaulay graphically explains

the step-by-step process in the construction of the Great
Pyramid by illustrating each phase with drawings.

Robert Pateman, *Egypt.* New York: Marshall Cavendish,
1993. A book from the Cultures of the World series about
Egyptians and their history.

Brenda Smith, *Egypt of the Pharaohs.* San Diego: Lucent
Books, 1996. A detailed and informative book for young
adults about ancient Egypt.

WORKS CONSULTED

E. A. Wallis Budge, *The Nile*. London: Thomas Cook & Son, 1912. This book about ancient Egypt was written by the keeper of the Egyptian and Assyrian antiquities at the British Museum. First published in the late 1890s, this book was meant to be a tourist guide for nineteenth-century travelers to Egypt.

Kathy Hansen, *Egypt Handbook*. Chico, CA: Moon, 1990. A traveler's guide to Egypt with maps, customs, and other details of modern Egypt.

Herodotus, *History*. Chicago: University of Chicago Press, 1987. A book first published in the fifth century B.C. by the Greek historian who explored the ancient Egyptian culture in great detail.

Edward William Lane, *An Account of the Manners and Customs of the Modern Egyptians*. New York: Dover, 1973. This book gives a detailed look into nineteenth-century Egyptian culture and society. It was originally published in 1836 by a British author in Egypt when the country was still under Turkish-Ottoman rule.

Leanne Logan et al., *Egypt*. Hawthorn, Australia: Lonely Planet, 1996. A traveler's guide to Egypt.

Timothy Mitchell, *Colonising Egypt*. Cambridge: Cambridge University Press, 1988. A book by a British author that explores the often harsh regimen imposed on most Egyptians when Great Britain ruled Egypt from 1882 to 1952.

Louis R. Mortimer, ed., *Egypt: A Country Study*. Washington, DC: Library of Congress, 1991. One of a large series of country studies published by the U.S. government that explores Egypt's history, government, economy, and culture in great detail.

Malise Ruthven, *Cairo*. Amsterdam: Time-Life International, 1980. This book was written for Time-Life's Great Cities series. It features good photos and an easy-to-read text that delves into the everyday lives of average Egyptians.

"Yellow Press: Egypt," *Economist,* March 28, 1998. An article about press censorship as practiced by the Egyptian government.

INDEX

Abu Simbel, temple of, 13

Account of the Manners and Customs of the Modern Egyptians, An (Lane), 17

agriculture
  in modern Egypt, 68, 86
  along Nile River, 20

Ahmad Fuad (King Fuad I), 53

al-Aqqad, Abbas Mahmud, 75

Al-Azhar University, 74

Alexander the Great, 35
  death of, 37

Alexandria, 15
  as center of trade, 42
  founding of Christian church in, 30
  library at, 39
  Muslim conquest of, 41

Al-Fustat (Cairo), 41

Al Hizb al Watani al Ahli (National Popular Party), 50

Al-Jihad (Holy War), 82

Amenophis III (queen), 34

Amr ibn al-As, 41

Anglo-Egyptian Agreement, 57

Antony, Mark, 38

Antony and Cleopatra (Shakespeare), 40

Anubis, 26

Arabian Desert, 8

Arab League, 60, 62

assassins, 43

Aswan Dam, 11–12

Aswan High Dam, 11, 13
  drawbacks of, 14
  Soviet support of, 59, 60

Augustus (Octavian), 38

Ayyubids, 44

Bast, 26

Bedouins, 12, 16, 17–18

Begin, Menachem, 62

Bent Pyramid, 27

Berbers, 16, 18

bilharzia, 72

Blue Nile, 9

Bonaparte, Napoléon, 45, 48, 82

Book of the Dead, 25

British
  Egypt under, 51–54
  in Tripartite Invasion, 59–60

Budge, E. A. Wallis, 25

Byzantine Empire, 40–41

Caesar, Julius, 38

Cairo, 15, 44, 69
  as center of learning, 43
  construction of, 30
  Muslim conquest of, 41

Cairo University, 74

Caisse de la Dette Publique (Bank Office of the Public Debt), 50

caliphs, 41

Camp David Accords, 62–63

Carter, Jimmy, 62

Champollion, Jean-François, 22

Cheops (Khufu), 27

  temple of, 30

Christianity

  introduction of, into Egypt, 40

Cleopatra VII, 38

  death of, 40

coffeehouses, 76

Cold War, 54

Colonising Egypt (Mitchell), 50

Colossi of Memnon, 34

Coptic Christians (Copts),
  16–17, 40

  in modern Egypt, 67

crime

  in modern Egypt, 82–83, 85

Darwich, Sayed, 74

Description de l'Egypte, 48

diet, 33

  in modern Egypt, 77–78

Djoser (king), 27

drug use

  in modern Egypt, 85

Eastern Desert, 15

education, 72–74

Egypt

  under British Empire, 51–54

  censorship in, 81

  First and Second Dynasties, 21

  Late Period, 34–35

  modernization of, 49

  Napoléon's conquest of,
    45–46

  Old and Middle Kingdoms,
    23–24

  under Ottoman Empire, 44–45

  under Roman rule, 40–41

  roots of civilization in, 20

  size and geography, 8

  Third Dynasty, 27

  traditional clothing in, 70

  Twelfth Dynasty, 24

  unification of, under Menes,
    20–21

Egypt (Logan et al.), 69

Egypt: A Country Study
  (Mortimer), 45, 53–54, 58

Egyptian Handbook (Hansen), 48

environment

  challenges of 21st century, 89

  effects of Aswan High Dam, 14

Farouk (king), 54

  overthrow of, 56

Fatimids, 42

Fuad I (king), 53

fellahin, 68

folk art, 76

Free Officers, 56

Gaza Strip, 56

Giza

  pyramids at, 27–29

government structure

  judicial system 81–82

  legislature, 80–81

  presidency, 80

Great Pyramid at Giza, 27

Great Sphinx, 29

Greece, 34, 36

  cultural influences of, 37–38

Hamito-Semitic race, 16

Hansen, Kathy, 48

Hathor, 26

health care, 72

Herodotus, 6, 27

hieroglyphs, 22

Hussein, Saddam, 64

Hyksos, 24

  routing of, 32

Imhotep, 27

industrial production, 86–87

International Conference on
  Population and Development
  in Cairo, 19

Isis, 26

Islam

  call to prayer, 66

  in daily life, 65

  dietary rules under, 78

  introduction of, into
    Egypt, 41

  sects of, 42

Islamic Jihad, 63

Islamic law *(Shari'a)*, 81

Israel

  creation of, as state, 56

  1967 attack on Egypt, 60–61

  occupation of Sinai by, 59

  Yom Kippur attack on, 61–62

Jama'ah al-Islamiyah (Islamic
  Group), 82

Julius Caesar (Shakespeare), 40

Karnak, temple of (at Thebes), 33

Khedive Ismail, 47, 49

Khedive Tawfiq, 50, 51

Koran, 65

  dietary rules under, 78

  on status of women, 70

Kulthum, Umm, 74

Lane, Edward William, 17

leisure activities, 76–77

Lesseps, Ferdinand-Marie de, 10

library at Alexandria, 39

literacy, 72

Libya, 64

Logan, Leanne, 69

Luxor, 15, 34

  terrorist attack at, 84

Mahfouz, Naguib, 75

Mamluks, 44

  power struggle with Ottomans,
    45, 46

Mark (Saint), 40

Mecca, 44

Medina, 44

Meidum pyramid, 27

Meketre at Deir el-Bahri, tomb
  of, 31–32

melayas (garment), 18

Menes (king), 22

  unification of Egypt under,
    20–21

Middle Kingdom, 23–24

minarets, 65–66

Mitchell, Timothy, 50

Mohammed Abd El Wahab, 74

Mortimer, Louis R., 45, 53, 58

Mubarak, Hosni, 63, 80, 82, 85

  role of, in Gulf War, 64

muezzin, 65–66

Muhammad (prophet), 41

Muhammad Ali Pasha, 46–47

mummification, 32

Muslim fundamentalists, 63

Napoleonic law, 82

Narmer (Menes), 22

Nasser, Gamal Abdel, 10, 58, 60, 85
  death of, 61
  forms Nonalignment Movement, 57, 59
  in 1952 revolution, 56
Nasser, Lake, 13
Nelson, Horatio (Lord), 46
New Kingdom, 32–35
  temple building during, 34
Nile, The (Budge), 25
Nile River, 9–11
  bond with early Egyptians, 20
1956 War, 59
nomarchs (governors), 24
Nonalignment Movement, 57, 59
Nubians, 18, 41
Nuqrashi, Mahmud, 55

oases, 12
Old Kingdom, 23–24
  pyramid building in, 27–30
Osiris, 25, 26
Ottoman Empire, 44–45

Palestine
  annexation of, 33
  partition of, 56
Palestine Liberation Organization (PLO), 60, 64
Persians, 34, 41
  defeat of, by Alexander the Great, 36
pharaonic system, 21
Philae, temple of, 13
Political Islam movement, 82
population growth, 19
Port Said, 15
Ptolemy, 37

Ptolemy XIII, 38
Ptolemy XIV, 38
Ptolemy XV, 38
  death of, 38
Pyramid Age, 27
Pyramids, Battle of the, 45

Qattara Depression, 8

Rahman, Omar Abdel, 82
Ramadan, 67
Red Pyramid, 27
Revolutionary Command Council (RCC), 56
Revolution of 1919, 52–53
Revolution of 1952, 56, 85
Roman Empire, 34
  rule of Egypt by, 40–41
Rommel, Erwin, 55
Rosetta Stone, 22
Ruthven, Malise, 66

Sadat, Anwar, 61, 62
  assassination of, 62
Sahara, 8
Said Pasha, 47
savants, 48
Selim I (the Grim), 44
Shakespeare, William, 40
Shalhoubi, Michael, 75
Shari'a (Islamic law), 81
Sharif, Omar, 75
Shiite Muslims, 42
Siwa, 16
Six-Day War, 60
Soviet Union, 55, 61
  Suez Canal construction and, 59
Sphinx, Great, 29

sports, 77

Step Pyramid, 27

Suez Canal, 10, 55, 86
  attempt to nationalize, 59
  building of, 47–48
  Ottoman-German attack on, 52

Sunni Muslims, 42

Syria
  annexation of, 33
  in Six-Day War, 60

temples
  Abu Simbel, 13
  Cheops, 30
  Karnak at Thebes, 33
  Philae, 13

Thebes, 34
  temple of Karnak at, 33

tourism, 87–88

trade
  Alexandria as center of, 42–43
  and population mix of Egypt, 16

via Suez Canal, 10, 38

Tripartite Invasion, 59

Tutankhamen, 33, 34

United Nations, 56

wadis (ravines), 8

Wafd (nationalist delegation),
  52–53

Western Desert, 15, 18

White Nile, 9

wildlife, 14

Winloch, Herbert, 30, 31

women, 67
  in modern Egypt, 69–71
  protest against British
    occupation by, 53

World War I, 52

World War II, 54, 55

Yom Kippur War, 61

PICTURE CREDITS

Cover photo: © Tony Stone Images/Ary Diesendruck
Art Resource, 22
The British Museum, 26
Classic Graphics, Egyptian Art, 24
Corbis, 58
Corbis/Bettmann, 39, 42, 44
Corbis/Reuters, 66, 75, 83
Egyptian Tourist Authority/Al-Ahram, 29
FPG International, 12, 14, 15, 16, 18, 37, 47, 64, 68, 71, 80,
    84, 88, 89
Grant Smith/Corbis, 13
Jimmy Carter Library, 62, 63
Library of Congress, 7, 21, 28, 30, 31
Lineworks, Inc., 9
North Wind Picture Archives, 40, 45
Photo Archive of Famous Places of the World, Dover
    Publications, Inc., 35
Scala/Art Resource, 27
UPI/Corbis-Bettmann, 51, 52, 73

ABOUT THE AUTHOR

Stuart A. Kallen is the author of more than 140 nonfiction books for children and young adults. He has written on topics ranging from the theory of relativity to rock-and-roll history to life on the American frontier. In addition, Mr. Kallen has written award-winning children's videos and television scripts. In his spare time, Mr. Kallen is a singer-songwriter-guitarist in San Diego, California.